State Fairs
& Church Bazaars

STELLA PARTON

Blue Ribbon Winning
& Family Specialties

State Fairs & Church Bazaars
Published by Attic Entertainment

© 2013 Attic Entertainment
P.O. Box 120871
Nashville, TN 37212
www.stellaparton.com
(615) 924-6284

ISBN: 0615756875
ISBN-13: 9780615756875
Library of Congress Control Number: 2013901188
Attic Entertainment, Nashville, Tennessee

Acknowledgments

I wish to thank Brenda L. Madden for her hard work in transcribing the submitted recipes from all of our contributors. She patiently endured all my suggestions. Thanks to Tim, for his suggestions after reading the first rough version and for being a willing taste-tester all these years. Thanks to Cindy Otto for her professional editing assistance. Thanks to Cyndi Hornsby for her photography. She always makes me look better than I do. Special thanks to Richard Trest at Ri'chard's Louisiana Café. Most importantly, thanks to the recipe contributors, without whom there would be no cookbook. We kept your recipes as close as possible to what you submitted. Thanks to all my family and friends who served as willing guinea pigs for all my cooking concoctions--you've been so brave. Last but not least, I would like to thank those of you who, like myself, collect cookbooks. We are in a club of our own.

The Blessing

God, thank you for this opportunity to be together and to share this wonderful meal before us. Bless this food to nourish our bodies. Remind us to always be grateful for the gifts you bestow. Help us remember to always share in a spirit of love. Amen.

Table of Contents

Introduction   1

Equivalent Chart   3

Substitution for Missing Ingredients   6

A Handy Spice & Herb Guide   8

Appetizers & Beverages   11

Breads   31

Soups & Salads   67

Meats   93

Vegetables   133

Pasta   173

Desserts   191

Contributors   303

Credits   309

Index   311

Introduction

While growing up in the mountains of East Tennessee, my fondest memories are of church picnics, covered dish suppers, church bazaars and county fairs. Memories of prize-winning home canned foods, beautiful cakes, pies, and all manner of delectable creations sporting shiny blue ribbons elicit warm feelings even now.

Collecting these tried and true recipes from the state fairs and churches has been an enjoyable experience. Your enthusiastic contributions to our newest collection of recipes, *"State Fairs & Church Bazaars"* still astounds me.

I began collecting recipes when I was nine or ten years old. As I visited county fairs, churches and concerts recipes seemed to find their way into my hands. After years of collecting dust in the back of a closet, these recipes are seeing the light of day in this cookbook.

Traveling around the world, I learned quickly that speaking of food was like a universal language. Everyone eats and people always have that as the basis for conversation. Many of my closest friendships developed this way.

Dinah Shore gave me my first live television cooking opportunity in the late seventies. Later, I appeared on Vicki Lawrence's show with Roger Clinton—President Clinton's brother.

In what seemed to be a trend, I cooked on *Live with Regis & Kathie Lee*, Lorianne Crook's *Celebrity Kitchen* and numerous regional and national TV shows across the country. I even did Minute Rice and General Foods spots for TNN's cooking shows.

Maybe, one day I can do a cookin' show from my own kitchen with friends and neighbors just dropping in.

I published my first cookbook nearly twenty years ago. The purpose of that cookbook was to raise money for charity. Since that first foray into "recipe rustling," I have stuck with the original plan by contributing funds from the sale of our cookbooks to many organizations. Typically, we donate to orphanages and Women and Children's Shelters.

This collection of recipes was contributed by many of you. We worked hard adjusting and correcting things to improve understandability for novices. Other than that, we left the recipes alone.

There are many country terms and old-fashioned words that may be unfamiliar. I left those alone to give "flavor" to the recipes. I view cooking as an art instead of a science so I try to keep the books non-technical. I love to cook and that is the only ingredient you need to get going in any kitchen, plus a good skillet, knife, a few good bowls, and a hot dependable stove.

Thanks for buying the cookbook.

Stella parton

Equivalent Chart

3 teaspoons	1 tablespoon
2 tablespoons	⅛ cup
4 tablespoons	¼ cup
8 tablespoons	½ cup
16 tablespoons	1 cup
5 tablespoons + 1 teaspoon	⅓ cup
12 tablespoons	¾ cup
4 ounces	½ cup
8 ounces	1 cup
16 ounces	1 pound
1 ounce	2 tablespoons fat or liquid
2 cups	1 pint
2 pints	1 quart
1 quart	4 cups
⅝ cup	¼ cup + 2 tablespoons
⅞ cup	¾ cup + 2 tablespoons
1 jigger	1 ½ fluid ounces (3 tablespoons)
8-10 egg whites	1 cup
12-14 egg yolks	1 cup
1 cup unwhipped cream	2 cups whipped
1 pound shredded American cheese	4 cups
¼ pound crumbled blue cheese	1 cup
1 lemon	3 tablespoons juice
1 orange	⅓ cup juice
1 pound unshelled walnuts	1 ¼ -1 ½ cup shelled
2 cups fat	1 pound
1 pound butter	2 cups or 4 sticks
2 cups granulated sugar	1 pound
3 ½ - 4 cups unsifted confectioners' sugar	1 pound

2 ¼ cups packed brown sugar	1 pound
4 cups sifted flour	1 pound
4 ½ cups cake flour	1 pound
3 ½ cups unsifted whole wheat flour	1 pound
4 ounces (1-1 ¼ cups) uncooked macaroni	2 ¼ cups cooked
7 ounces spaghetti	4 cups cooked
4 ounces (1 ½ -2 cups) uncooked noodles	2 cups cooked
28 saltine crackers	1 cup crumbs
4 slices bread	1 cup crumbs
14 square graham crackers	1 cup crumbs
22 vanilla wafers	1 cup crumbs

General Oven Chart

Very slow oven	250°F-300°F
Slow oven	300°F-325°F
Moderate oven	325°F-375°F
Medium hot oven	375°F-400°F
Hot oven	400°F-450°F
Very hot oven	450°F-500°F

Contents of Cans

Of the different sizes of cans used by commercial canners, the most common are:

Size	Average Contents
8 ounces	1 cup
Picnic	1 ¼ cups
No. 300	1 ¾ cups
No. 1 tall	2 cups
No. 303	2 cups
No. 2	2 ½ cups
No. 2 ½	3 ½ cups
No. 3	4 cups
No. 10	12-13 cups

Substitutions for a Missing Ingredient

1 cup sour milk = 1 cup sweet milk with 1 tablespoon vinegar or lemon juice stirred in.

1 cup sweet milk = 1 cup sour milk or buttermilk and ½ teaspoon baking soda

1 square chocolate (1 ounce) = 3-4 tablespoon cocoa and ½ tablespoon fat

1 tablespoon cornstarch (for thickening) = 2 tablespoons flour

1 cup sifted all-purpose flour = 1 cup and 2 tablespoons sifted cake flour

1 cup sifted cake flour = 1 cup minus 2 tablespoons sifted all-purpose flour

1 teaspoon baking powder = ¼ teaspoon baking soda plus ½ teaspoon cream of tartar

¾ cup cracker crumbs = 1 cup bread crumbs

1 cup heavy sour cream = ⅓ cup butter and ⅔ cup milk in any sour milk recipe

1 teaspoon dried herbs = 1 tablespoon fresh herbs

1 cup whole milk = ½ cup evaporated milk and ½ cup water

or 1 cup reconstituted nonfat dry milk and 1 tablespoon butter

2 ounces compressed yeast = 3 (¼-ounce) packets of dry yeast

1 tablespoon prepared mustard = 1 teaspoon dry mustard

⅛ teaspoon garlic powder = 1 small pressed garlic clove

1 pound whole dates = 1 ½ cups, pitted and cut

3 medium bananas = 1 cup mashed

3 cups dry corn flakes = 1 cup crushed

10 miniature marshmallows = 1 large marshmallow

1 tablespoon instant minced onion, rehydrated = 1 small fresh onion

A Handy Spice & Herb Guide

ALLSPICE - a pea-sized fruit that grows in Mexico, Jamaica, Central and South America. Its delicate flavor resembles a blend of cloves, cinnamon and nutmeg. Uses: Whole - pickles, meats, boiled fish, gravies; Ground - puddings, relishes, fruit preserves, baking.

BASIL - the dried leaves and stems of an herb grown in the United States and North Mediterranean area. Has an aromatic, leafy flavor. Uses: For flavoring tomato dishes and tomato paste, turtle soup; also use in cooked peas, squash, snap beans, sprinkle chopped over lamb chops and poultry.

BAY LEAVES - the dried leaves of an evergreen grown in the eastern Mediterranean countries. Has a sweet, herbaceous floral spice note. Uses: For pickling, stews, for spicing sauces and soup. Also use with a variety of meats and fish.

CARAWAY - the seed of a plant grown in the Netherlands. Flavor that combines the tastes of Anise and Dill. Uses: For the cordial Kummel, baking breads; often added to sauerkraut, noodles, cheese spreads. Also adds zest to French fried potatoes, liver, canned asparagus.

CURRY POWDER - a ground blend of ginger, turmeric, fenugreek seed, as many as 16 to 20 spices. Uses: For all Indian curry recipes such as lamb, chicken, and rice, eggs, vegetables, and curry puffs.

DILL - the small, dark seed of the dill plant grown in India, having a clean, aromatic taste. Uses: Dill is a predominant seasoning in pickling recipes; also adds pleasing flavor to sauerkraut, potato salad, cooked macaroni, and green apple pie.

MACE - the dried covering around the nutmeg seed. Its flavor is similar to nutmeg, but with a fragrant, delicate difference. Uses: Whole - for picklin', fish, fish sauce, and stewed fruit; Ground - delicious in baked goods, pastries and doughnuts, adds unusual flavor to chocolate desserts.

MARJORAM - an herb of the mint family, grown in France and Chile. Has a minty-sweet flavor. Uses: In beverages, jellies and to flavor soups, stews, fish, sauces. Also, excellent to sprinkle on lamb while roasting.

MSG (Monosodium Glutamate) - is a vegetable protein derivative for raising the effectiveness of natural food flavors. Uses: Small amounts, adjusted to individual taste, can be added to steaks, roasts, chops, seafoods, stews, soups, chowder, chop suey and cooked vegetables.

OREGANO - a plant of the mint family and a species of marjoram of which the dried leaves are used to make an herb seasoning. Uses: An excellent flavoring for any tomato dish, especially pizza, chili con carne, and Italian specialties.

PAPRIKA - a mild, sweet red pepper growing in Spain, Central Europe and the United States. Slightly aromatic and prized for brilliant red color. Uses: A colorful garnish for pale foods, and for seasoning chicken paprika, Hungarian goulash, salad dressings.

POPPY - the seed of a flower grown in Holland. Has a rich fragrance and crunchy, nut-like flavor. Uses: Excellent as a topping for breads, rolls and cookies. Also delicious in buttered noodles.

ROSEMARY - an herb (like a curved pine needle) grown in France, Spain, and Portugal, and having a sweet, fresh taste. Uses: In lamb dishes, in soups, stews and to sprinkle on beef before roasting.

SAGE - the leaf of a shrub grown in Greece, Yugoslavia and Albania. Flavor is camphoraceous and minty. Uses: For meat and poultry stuffing, sausages, meatloaf, hamburgers, stews and salads.

THYME - the leaves and stems of a shrub grown in France and Spain. Has a strong, distinctive flavor. Uses: For poultry seasoning, in croquettes, fricassees and fish dishes. Also tasty on fresh sliced tomatoes.

TURMERIC - a root of the ginger family, grown in India, Haiti, Jamaica and Peru, having a mild, ginger-pepper flavor. Uses: As a flavoring and coloring in prepared mustard and in combination with mustard as a flavoring for meats, dressings, salads.

Appetizers
& Beverages

Lemonade

2 lemons
2 cups sugar
1 gallon water

Cut bad places or print off lemon, if any. Wash and cut lemon in half. Juice lemons. Remove seeds. Cut rinds in small pieces. Mix rinds, juice, sugar and water in gallon-sized container. Stir. Add more water. Mix until all water is added. Recipe may be reduced by half to make half-gallon serving.

Edna Shaw, Grace United Methodist Church,
Three Springs, PA

Banana Frost

1 ripe banana
½ cup orange juice
½ cup milk
1 pint orange sherbet

Peel and slice banana. Place in blender and mash. Add orange juice until smooth. Add milk and half of orange sherbet. Blend until smooth. Pour into glasses. Top with scoop of orange sherbet and banana slices if desired.

Cranberry Orange Punch

2 bottles (32-ounces each) cranberry juice cocktail, chilled
1 ½ cups lemon juice from concentrate
⅔ cup sugar
2 cans (12-ounces each) orange soda, chilled
½ cup orange flavor liqueur, optional

In large punch bowl, combine both juices and sugar. Stir until sugar dissolves. Just before serving, add orange soda, liqueur if desired, and ice. Garnish if desired. Makes 3 ½ quarts.

Fruit Juice Cooler

2 bottles (6 ½-ounces each) sparkling mineral water, chilled
1 can (12-ounce) peach nectar, chilled
½ cup unsweetened orange juice, chilled
¼ cup unsweetened grapefruit juice, chilled
2 tablespoons lemon juice, chilled

Combine all ingredients in a large pitcher. Mix well. Pour over ice cubes in serving glasses. Serve immediately.

Wassail

2 gallons sweet apple cider
1 cup pineapple juice
2 cups orange juice
1 cup lemon juice
1 cup sugar
1 stick whole cinnamon
1 teaspoon whole cloves

Combine all the ingredients and bring to a simmer. Strain and serve hot.

"This is a great Christmas treat and will help with your holiday entertaining."

Sparkling Harves Cider

2 quarts apple cider (or juice)
1 cup lemon juice from concentrate
½ cup sugar
1 bottle (32-ounce) ginger ale

In punch bowl combine cider, lemon juice, and sugar. Stir until sugar dissolves. Chill. Just before serving add ginger ale. Serve over ice. Makes 3 quarts.

Cranberry Tea

8 cups water
1 cinnamon stick
12 whole allspice
4 cloves
3 tea bags
1 cup sugar
1 cup orange juice
¼ cup lemon juice
1 quart cranberry juice

In a large stock pot, boil 5 cups of water with cinnamon, allspice, cloves and tea bags. Let ingredients steep for 5 minutes. Remove the cinnamon, allspice, cloves and tea bags and discard. Add the sugar, orange juice, lemon juice, cranberry juice and the remaining 3 cups of hot water. Serve hot or cold.

Vegetable Dip

1 medium onion
½ teaspoon hot sauce
2 teaspoons vegetable dip mix
2 cups mayonnaise
2 cups small curd cottage cheese
1 crushed garlic clove
1 teaspoon salt

Mix all ingredients in blender or mix with rotary mixer until smooth. Chill until ready to serve with vegetable sticks.

Mexican Bean Dip

1 can (15-ounce) red kidney beans, rinsed and drained
1 medium avocado, chopped
2 tablespoons lemon juice
2 tablespoons tomato paste
1 red chili, finely chopped
2 cloves garlic, minced
1 tablespoon sugar substitute
1 green onion, sliced
¼ cup parsley, chopped

Process kidney beans, avocado, lemon juice, tomato paste, chili, garlic and sugar substitute in food processor until well blended. Stir in green onion and 3 tablespoons parsley. Sprinkle with remaining parsley.

Judy Heath, Cornerstone Baptist Church,
Macon, GA

Swiss Fondue

¾ pound Swiss cheese
1 tablespoon all-purpose flour
1 ¼ cloves garlic
1 ¼ cups white wine
Dash of pepper
Dash of nutmeg
Salt to taste

Cut cheese into thin strips and place in a bag. Add the flour and toss well until cheese is coated. Split the garlic clove in half and rub the inside of the fondue pot well with the cut sides of both halves. Press the remaining ¼ clove of garlic with a garlic press and place in the fondue pot, then add the wine. Place over the flame and heat until bubbles start to rise. Do not cover or boil. Add the cheese gradually and cook over a low flame, stirring constantly, until melted. Stir in the pepper and nutmeg. If the mixture gets too thick, you may add warm white wine. Serve with French bread cubes, cauliflowerets, mushrooms and rolled pepperoni slices for dipping.

Hot Garlic & Anchovy Dip

2 cups heavy cream
4 tablespoons butter
8 flat anchovy fillets, drained, rinsed and finely chopped
1 teaspoon finely chopped garlic

Reduce cream by bringing to a boil in heavy saucepan, cooking and stirring frequently for 15-20 minutes. Reduce to about 1 cup. In 3-4 cups flameproof casserole or fondue pot, melt butter over low heat. Add anchovies and garlic, then the reduced cream. Bring to a simmer, stirring constantly. Do not let boil. Serve at once, keeping warm over candle warmer or sterno burner. Serves 6. Serve with Italian bread sticks or vegetable strips.

Southwest Vegetable Dip

1 small can chopped black olives
2 tomatoes, peeled & chopped
2 tablespoons olive oil
Salt to taste
1 small can chopped chilies
6-8 green onions with tops, chopped
1 tablespoon vinegar

Make sure the olives and chilies are drained and squeeze out excess juice from the tomato. Mix ingredients together and serve with nacho chips.

Party Bean Dip

1 can chili (no beans)
1 can refried beans
½ package cheddar cheese (cut up or shredded)
1 bag nacho chips

Mix chili, refried beans and cheese in saucepan. Heat over low-medium heat until cheese is melted. Keep on low heat or in a fondue. Serve with nachos.

Jalapeño Wheat Cheese Rolls

1 ½ cups warm water
3 tablespoons sugar
3 teaspoons yeast
1 ½ teaspoons salt
3 cups flour
1 cup white wheat flour
1 egg
3 tablespoons margarine or oil
3 cups Mexican cheese
1 ½ cups onion chopped
1 tablespoon salt free seasoning
6 jalapeños, chopped

Garnish
Egg wash
Sesame seeds
6 jalapeños, chopped

Preheat oven to 350°F. In a large bowl combine water and sugar to dissolve. Sprinkle yeast over top of water. Add flours 1 cup at a time. Add remaining ingredients. Beat until smooth. Continue adding flour to make a soft dough. Cover and let rise in warm place until doubled. When dough is ready, roll out into a large rectangle. Spread with cheese, onion, jalapeños and seasoning. Roll up tightly. Cut into slices or triangles. Line a 12-inch Dutch oven with parchment paper. Place rolls immediately into greased Dutch oven. Brush with egg and sprinkle sesame seeds and jalapeños. Let rise again until almost doubled. Bake for about 25-30 minutes. Allow to cool a little and serve.

Rosa and Marisela Sanchez, Utah State Fair,
Salt Lake City, UT

Salsa Reynolds

1 can chopped pineapple, drained
8 tomatoes
1 red onion
1 bunch cilantro
5 garlic cloves
1 lime, juiced
1 yellow bell pepper, chopped
1 jalapeño, diced
Salt to taste
Cinnamon to taste
Cumin to taste
Avocado, peeled and mashed

Combine all ingredients in a medium mixing bowl. Serve with your favorite tortilla chips.

Bob & Becky Reynolds, Utah State Fair,
Salt Lake City, UT

Smokin' Salsa

5 tomatoes
1 large onion
1 Anaheim pepper
3 jalapeños
2 Seron peppers
½ cup celery
¼ cup oil
2 tablespoons red wine vinegar
1 teaspoon coriander, crushed
1 teaspoon mustard seed
1 teaspoon salt
Pepper to taste

Preheat oven to 350°F. Cut tomatoes and onion into large pieces. Roast tomatoes and onion in oven for approximately 20-25 minutes until edges are burnt. Chop peppers, jalapeños and celery. Add remaining ingredients and mix. Refrigerate before serving.

John Shimota, Dakota County Fair,
Farmington, MN

Marinated Cheese

½ cup olive oil
⅜ cup red wine vinegar
⅛ cup Balsamic vinegar
3 tablespoons minced fresh parsley
3 tablespoons minced green onions
3 garlic cloves, minced
1 teaspoon dried basil
¼ teaspoon salt
¼ teaspoon pepper
2 packages (8-ounces each) cream cheese

Combine the first 9 ingredients in a medium mixing bowl. Cut 2 bricks of cream cheese into ½-inch cubes. Pour marinade over cubes of cheese. Let stand at room temperature for 90 minutes, and then chill. Remove from refrigerator 30 minutes prior to eating. Serve with your favorite cracker.

Dakota County Fair, Farmington, MN

Breads

Iron Skillet Cornbread

1 cup coarse cornmeal
¼ cup flour
1 teaspoon baking powder
Dash salt
1 tablespoon cooking oil
Milk (to desired batter)

Preheat oven to 375°F. Mix ingredients to desired batter. Pour into greased skillet and bake until top is golden. Serve hot. Large skillet makes thin cornbread or medium skillet makes thick cornbread.

The Most Delicious Rolls You've Tasted

1 cup margarine (do not use butter)
1 cup cold milk
¼ cup sugar
2 eggs
1 package yeast, dissolved in ¼ cup warm water
1 teaspoon salt
4 ½-5 cups flour, separated into 3 cups plus 1 ½-2 cups

Preheat oven to 350°F. Heat margarine only to melt. Add milk, sugar, eggs, dissolved yeast, salt and 3 cups flour. Mix well and add remaining flour. Cover and refrigerate overnight. Make into rolls by dividing into 3 sections. Roll out each into about 12-inch circle. Divide into 12 sections like pie pieces. Roll up starting with the large end, make sure point is on the bottom and place on well-greased pan. Cover and let rise until doubled. Bake about 10-20 minutes or until as brown as you like. This dough will keep several days the refrigerator or the baked rolls freeze very well. The dough is sticky after mixing but handles well when cold. Other flour may be used in place of ½ - 1 cup flour.

Larry & Brenda Wisse, Trinity Lutheran Church, Marysville, OH

Cinnamon Apple Muffins

2 cups flour, sifted
1 tablespoon baking powder
1 ½ teaspoons cinnamon
⅓ cup sugar
1 teaspoon salt
1 egg, beaten
¾ cup milk
3 tablespoons solid vegetable shortening, melted
1 cup apples, unpeeled, grated

Preheat oven to 350°F. Mix dry ingredients in bowl. Mix egg, milk, shortening and apples in another bowl; add apple mixture to dry ingredients. Mix lightly only until moist. Pour into well-greased muffin tins. Sprinkle topping on top. Bake 20-25 minutes.

Croutons

2 loaves of bread
5-7 cloves garlic
1 ½ cups virgin olive oil
1 cup fresh grated brick parmesan cheese
1 ½ tablespoons Hungarian paprika
1 tablespoon thyme leaves
½ tablespoon turkey seasoning
½ tablespoon chicken seasoning
½ teaspoon herbed pepper
½ tablespoon basil leaves
½ tablespoon tarragon leaves
½ tablespoon oregano leaves

Cut bread into 1-inch squares. Put garlic cloves and virgin olive oil in a large skillet. Heat to medium-high then add bread pieces. Sauté until dark brownish black and crispy. Spatula croutons and garlic pieces into brown paper bag containing spices. Shake bag. Pour bag contents into Caesar salad and toss.

Southern Cracklin' Bread

2 cups self-rising cornmeal
½ teaspoon salt
1 ½ cups buttermilk
2 tablespoons solid vegetable shortening, melted
1 teaspoon sugar
1 ½ cups cracklings
1 tablespoon flour

Preheat oven to 450°F. Mix all ingredients well. Put into pan. Pour fried meat (bacon) drippings on top and bake for 30-40 minutes until done.

Judy Heath, Cornerstone Baptist Church,
Macon, GA

Blueberry Sour Cream Corn Muffins

1 cup all-purpose flour
¾ cup cornmeal
2 teaspoons baking powder
1 teaspoon baking soda
¼ teaspoon salt
1 egg, beaten
1 cup reduced fat sour cream
⅓ cup frozen unsweetened apple juice concentrate, thawed
1 ½ cups fresh or frozen blueberries
⅔ cup reduced fat whipped cream cheese
2 tablespoons no-sugar-added blueberry fruit spread

Preheat oven to 400°F. Spray 12 muffin cups with cooking spray, or line with paper liners. Combine flour, cornmeal, baking powder, soda and salt in medium bowl. Add combined egg, sour cream and apple juice. Mix just until dry ingredients are moistened. Stir in blueberries. Spoon batter into prepared muffin cups. Bake 18-20 minutes or until brown. Let stand 5 minutes. Remove from pan. Cool slightly. Combine cream cheese and fruit spread. Serve with warm muffins.

Judy Heath, Cornerstone Baptist Church, Macon, GA

Crusty Garlic Bread

2 cloves garlic, minced
2 teaspoons olive oil
2 tablespoons chopped fresh parsley
2 tablespoons chopped fresh thyme (or 2 tablespoons dried thyme)
2 teaspoons chopped fresh marjoram (or ¾ teaspoon dried marjoram)
½ teaspoon paprika
2 tablespoons grated Parmesan cheese (optional)
2 small loaves (4-ounces each) Italian or French bread

Preheat oven to 350°F. In a small bowl, combine the garlic and oil; mix well. In another small bowl, combine parsley, thyme, marjoram, and paprika. Add Parmesan. Mix well. Cut each loaf crosswise into diagonal slices, without cutting all the way through. Brush cut sides of slices with garlic oil. Sprinkle herb mixture between slices. Wrap each loaf in foil; place on a baking sheet. Bake until heated through, about 10-15 minutes. Unwrap the loaves and place them on a breadboard or in a basket. Serve immediately.

Veggie Bars

2 cans (8-ounces each) crescent rolls
2 packages (8-ounces each) cream cheese, softened
¼ cup mayonnaise
1 package (1-ounce) ranch dressing mix
1 medium red pepper, diced
1 medium green pepper, diced
½ cup coarsely chopped broccoli flowerets
½ cup coarsely chopped mushroom
¾ cup shredded cheddar cheese

Preheat oven to 350°F. Unroll crescent dough. Place in lightly greased 15x10-inch jelly roll pan, pressing edges and perforations together to line bottom of pan. Bake for 7-8 minutes or until brown. Cool. Combine cream cheese, mayonnaise, and dressing mix. Beat on medium speed until smooth (1-1 ½ minutes). Spread over crust. Combine peppers and remaining ingredients. Sprinkle over cream cheese mixture. Cover and chill 8 hours. Cut into 2-inch squares.

Judy Heath, Cornerstone Baptist Church, Macon, GA

Iron Skillet Biscuits

2 cups self-rising flour
¼ cup solid vegetable shortening
1 cup buttermilk

Preheat oven to 450°F. Put flour in a large bowl. Cut in shortening with pastry blender or fork until consistency of cornmeal. Pour buttermilk into mixture. Stir with flour until dough is together. Turn out onto a floured surface. Knead gently for about ½ minute. Roll or pat dough to ½-inch thickness. Cut with a biscuit cutter or glass (rim dipped in flour first). Grease iron skillet with shortening. Place biscuits ½-inch apart. Bake for 10-12 minutes.

Easy Hot Rolls

1 cup solid shortening
1 tablespoon salt
½ cup sugar
2 cups boiling water
2 packages dry yeast
2 eggs, beaten
7 cups plain flour
Vegetable oil

Preheat oven to 400°F. Put first 3 ingredients in a mixing bowl. Add boiling water. Let cool to temperature of a baby's bottle. Mix yeast with ½ cup warm water (same temperature as mixture). Add eggs, then flour. If mixing with an electric mixer, add last cup of flour by hand (the more you mix the better they are). Rub a little vegetable oil over the dough; cover with a damp dishtowel, and refrigerate at least 6 hours. (Overnight will work!) Punch down the dough, then roll and cut using flour as needed to keep dough from sticking to the surface. Let rise 1-2 hours. Brush with butter if desired. Bake for 10 minutes. If you desire a square shaped roll, use a pizza cutter slightly oiled and floured to cut your rolls. Then bake on a cookie sheet.

Barbara Jarvis, Forest Heights Methodist Church, Jackson, TN

Jalapeño Cornbread

3 eggs, beaten
2 cups milk
1 small can hot chili peppers
½ cup oil
1 small can creamed corn
1 bunch green onions, chopped
3 cups self-rising cornmeal
½ teaspoon baking powder
½ teaspoon salt
1 tablespoon sugar
1 ½ cups grated cheddar cheese

Preheat oven to 350°F. In a mixing bowl, whip eggs and milk together. Add peppers, oil, corn, and onion. Next add cornmeal, baking powder, salt, and sugar. Mix well. Stir in grated cheese. Pour into a large well- greased oblong pan. Bake for approximately 45 minutes.

Note: This bread freezes well. Cut into squares. Wrap in foil to freeze.

Hush Puppies

1 cup buttermilk (not low fat)
½ cup cornmeal (yellow)
1 cup self-rising flour
3 teaspoons sugar
3 teaspoons baking powder
1 egg
4 slices of whole onion, chopped
1 can (11-ounce) whole kernel corn or jalapeño (drain water from the corn)

Mix all ingredients in a large bowl. Let rise (5-10 minutes). The batter should set up to a mortar or putty like consistency. If it's runny add some cornmeal and flour. Dip the hushpuppies with a candy dipper or small spoon and drop them in 375°F peanut oil. They should turn themselves over, but may not. Cook till golden brown, approximately 5 minutes.

Note: Make sure all liquids are drained from ingredients before adding.

John Shelton, Bells, TN

Cinnamon Rolls

<u>Rolls</u>
1 cup sugar, plus ¼ cup
2 tablespoons cinnamon
½ cup butter
1 teaspoon salt
1 egg
3 ½ - 3 ¾ cups all-purpose flour, separated into 2 cups and 1
½ - 1 ¾ cups
1 tablespoon active dry yeast
1 cup warm water (120°F)
3 tablespoons butter, melted

<u>Frosting</u>
1 ¼ cups confectioners' sugar
¼ teaspoon vanilla
1-2 tablespoons half & half

<u>For rolls</u>: Preheat oven to 325°F. In small bowl, combine the 1 cup sugar and cinnamon; set aside. In large bowl, cream the butter, remaining sugar and salt. Stir in egg, 2 cups of the flour and the yeast. Pour in water; mix well. Stir in 1 ½ - 1 ¾ cups flour.

Turn out onto lightly floured surface; knead until soft dough forms. Place in greased bowl, turning once to grease surface. Cover. Let rise until double. Roll out to 9x4-inch rectangle. Spread with melted butter. Sprinkle with cinnamon–sugar mixture. Roll up from long side; seal edge. Cut into 12 slices. Place, cut side up, in 3 greased 8x8-inch pans. Let rise until double. Bake in convection oven 16-17 minutes (350°F for 20-25 minutes for conventional oven). Remove from pans. Cool on wire racks. Frost when cool.

For frosting: Beat all ingredients until well mixed. Pour over top of rolls, adding more half and half if necessary.

Donna Summer, Iowa State Fair,
Des Moines, IA

French Toast

French bread (approximately 10-12 one inch slices)
1 package (3-ounce) low fat cream cheese
1 cup skim milk
⅓ cup maple syrup (pancake syrup)
3 eggs or egg substitute
2 tablespoons melted butter, margarine or butter substitute
1 tablespoon sugar
1 teaspoon cinnamon
1 teaspoon vanilla
¼ cup chopped nuts (optional)
1 can peaches, sliced and drained (or fresh apples)

Preheat oven to 400°F. Spread cream cheese on front and back of each slice of bread. Put in 9x13-inch sprayed pan. In a medium bowl mix the next seven ingredients with a whisk. Pour over bread. Can cover and refrigerate overnight. Just before baking, drain a can of peach slices (or use fresh apples) and place a slice on top of bread. Bake for 25-30 minutes until set.

Sandra Hill, Union Cumberland Presbyterian Church,
Farragut, TN

Biscuits

2 cups self-rising flour
⅛ cup solid vegetable shortening
⅛ cup butter
½ cup buttermilk
¼ cup whole milk

Preheat oven to 425°F. Sift flour into mixing bowl. Cut shortening and butter into flour with pastry blender. Add buttermilk and milk to mixture, stirring just enough to moisten flour. Turn onto floured surface. Pat with your hand into thickness desired. Cut with the biscuit cutter. Do not turn cutter. Place on pan and bake for 12 minutes, or until golden brown. The less the dough is handled, the better the biscuits.

John Spargo, Tennessee Valley Fair,
Knoxville, TN

Cranberry Bread

2 cups flour
¾ cup sugar
1 egg
⅔ cup milk
¼ cup butter
1 can whole cranberries
½ cup pecans or walnuts
Raisins, if desired

Preheat oven to 350°F. In a medium bowl, mix all ingredients. Pour into loaf pan. Cook for 1 hour.

Bonnie Youngblood,
Warrior, AL

Tomato Juice Bread

1 cup hot tomato juice
¼ cup sugar
1 tablespoon salt
1 ½ tablespoons solid vegetable shortening, plus extra for greasing pan
1 package (¼-ounce) dry yeast
¾ cup plus ¼ cup warm water
6 cups sifted flour

Combine tomato juice, sugar, salt and shortening, and stir until sugar dissolves. Cool to lukewarm. Activate yeast in ¼ cup warm water. Add yeast and remaining ¾ cup water to cooled tomato juice mixture. Add 3 cups flour, blending well. Gradually add enough remaining flour to make soft dough. Turn dough out onto lightly floured board and knead until smooth and elastic, 8-10 minutes. Form into smooth ball. Place in 2 greased 9x5-inch loaf pans. Cover and let rise in warm place free from drafts until doubled in bulk, about 1 hour. Bake at 400°F until toothpick inserted in center comes out clean, about 30 minutes. Remove from pans at once and cool.

"This recipe is fun, because not only does it have a unique flavor, but it brings back memories of a more secure world when home was where family and friends gathered around and Mother was in the kitchen creating her magic."

Renee Tener, Los Angeles, CA

Blueberry Muffins

5 tablespoons butter, melted
1 ¾ cups all-purpose flour
½ cup sugar
1 ½ teaspoons baking powder
½ teaspoon baking soda
¾ teaspoon cinnamon*
1 cup buttermilk
1 large egg
½ teaspoon vanilla extract
¾ teaspoon salt
1 cup blueberries

Preheat oven to 400°F. Grease 12 large muffin cups. Melt the butter and set it aside to cool slightly. Sift the flour, sugar, baking powder, baking soda and cinnamon into a bowl. Stir. Combine the buttermilk, egg, vanilla extract and melted butter in a second bowl. Beat the liquid ingredients to form a uniformly colored mixture. Pour the liquid ingredients into the dry ones. Stir only enough to moisten all the dry ingredients. DO NOT beat into a smooth batter; this makes the muffins tough. Fold in the blueberries. Fill the muffin cups ½ to ⅔ full with the batter.

Bake 20-25 minutes or until a cake tester inserted into the center comes out clean.

*Note: You can substitute 1 tablespoon freshly grated orange peel or 2 teaspoon freshly grated lemon rind for the cinnamon.

Spotted Seasoned Snakes

4-4 ½ cups flour, separated into 2 cups, 1 ½ cups and 1 cup
1 package rapid rise yeast
1 ¼ cups milk, warmed
¼ cup vegetable oil
¼ cup sugar
1 egg
1 teaspoon salt
1 teaspoon minced dried onion
½ teaspoon dill weed
½ teaspoon crushed dried oregano
¼ teaspoon garlic powder
1 teaspoon grated parmesan cheese
½ cup finely chopped pepperoni
½ cup shredded cheddar cheese
2 tablespoons melted butter
Poppy seeds
1 jar spaghetti sauce

Preheat oven to 350°F. In a large mixing bowl combine 2 cups flour, yeast, warm milk, oil, sugar, egg and salt. Beat with mixer for 3 minutes. Add 1 more cup of flour plus the onion, dill weed, oregano, garlic powder, and parmesan cheese. Stir by hand mixing all ingredients well. Turn out on floured pastry sheet. Add pepperoni and cheese. Add flour to make moderately stiff dough. Knead for 5 minutes. Place in a covered oiled bowl and let rise 20 minutes. Punch bread dough down. By hand roll 6-8-inch long ropes. Wrap ropes around a lightly greased 8-inch dowel rod. Place on a lightly greased 10x15-inch cookie sheet. Put whole cloves for the eyes and pieces of pepperoni for the tongue. Let rise until doubled in size. Brush snakes with melted butter and sprinkle poppy seed on top. Bake for 20 minutes. Makes 12-15 "snakes", depending on size. Serve warm dipped in warm spaghetti sauce.

Mary & Enoch Hardin, Utah State Fair,
Salt Lake City, UT

Cinnamon Apple Muffins

Muffins
2 cups flour, sifted
1 tablespoon baking powder
1 ½ teaspoons cinnamon
⅓ cup sugar
1 teaspoon salt
1 egg, beaten
¾ cup milk
3 tablespoons shortening, melted
1 cup apples, unpeeled, grated

Topping
½ cup nuts, chopped
½ teaspoon cinnamon
2 tablespoons brown sugar

For muffins: Preheat oven to 350°F. Mix dry ingredients in bowl. Mix egg, milk, shortening and apples in another bowl; add apple mixture to dry ingredients. Mix lightly only until moist. Pour into well-greased muffin tins. Sprinkle topping on top. Bake 20-25 minutes.

For topping: Mix together well. I prefer walnuts.

Onion or Cheddar Bread

2 loaves of frozen bread dough, thawed
1 cup cheddar cheese, grated
1 stick butter
1 package dry onion soup mix

Preheat oven to 350°F. Slice each loaf into 12 pieces. Flatten each piece of dough. Put grated cheese in center and roll dough into a ball keeping cheese inside of dough. Grease and flour pans. For onion flavors, melt butter and mix in dry onion soup mix. Roll dough balls into the mixture. Then put into pans to bake. Put into bundt pan or muffin pan. Bake for 25-30 minutes.

South of the Border Cornbread Bake

<u>Cornbread Batter</u>
1 package (6-ounce) Mexican style cornbread mix
½ can (14 ¾-ounce) cream style corn
1 egg, well beaten
1 tablespoon honey
½ cup milk

<u>Filling</u>
1 pound ground beef
1 large onion, chopped
1 large bell pepper, chopped
2 cloves garlic, minced
½ can (14 ½-ounce) diced tomatoes and green chilies
1 can (15 ½-ounce) kidney beans, drained
1 teaspoon chili powder (or more to taste)
½ teaspoon ground cumin
2 cups grated sharp cheddar cheese
Fresh cracked pepper

Preheat oven to 350°F. Mix together Mexican cornbread mix, ½ can cream style corn, egg, honey and milk. Blend well until the consistency of cake batter. Set aside. In a 10-inch or larger cast iron skillet, cook ground beef, onion, bell pepper, and garlic until browned. Pour through strainer to drain grease. Return to pan and add the other half of cream style corn, diced tomatoes and chilies, kidney beans, chili powder, and ground cumin. Cook an additional 5 minutes. Top the filling with the grated cheese. Pour the cornbread batter over the meat and cheese filling. Sprinkle with fresh cracked pepper. Bake for 45-50 minutes or until brown. Remove from oven and let cool 10 minutes before serving.

Petra Mitchell, Wilson County Fair,
Lebanon, TN

Basic White Bread

Bread
1 ½ cups lukewarm water
2 packages yeast
7 ½ cups all-purpose flour
3 tablespoons sugar
1 cup milk
1 tablespoon salt
¼ cup butter

Plain Bread Glaze
1 egg
1 teaspoon olive oil

Egg White Bread Glaze
1 egg white
Extra fine sugar

For Bread: Place lukewarm water in a large bowl or crock. Sprinkle the yeast over the water, stirring until dissolved. Cover and let stand 15 minutes. Combine 1 ½ cups flour and 2 tablespoons sugar. Beat the flour mixture carefully into the yeast mixture with a wooden spoon until free from lumps. Cover with a towel and let rise in a warm place for 30 minutes.

Scald the milk, then stir in the salt and remaining sugar. Add the butter and stir until dissolved. Cool to lukewarm. Add to the yeast mixture, then add enough of the remaining flour to make a soft dough.

Turn out on a lightly floured board and knead for about 10 minutes or until smooth and elastic, adding flour if needed. Place in a greased bowl, turning dough to grease the top. Cover with a towel and let rise in a warm place for an hour or until doubled in bulk. Turn dough out on a lightly floured board and divide in half. Shape into loaves and place in 2 well greased 9x5-inch loaf pans. Cover and let rise for an hour or until double in bulk.

Bake at 400°F for 25 minutes. (If you will be using one of the glazes, described below, on your bread, bake for 10 minutes then apply the glaze, then bake 15 minutes.) Turn loaves out on a wire rack to cool.

For Plain Bread Glaze: Combine the ingredients and beat well. Strain before using.

For Egg White Bread Glaze: Brush egg white over surface of bread and sprinkle with sugar.

Scones

2 cups baking mix
1 teaspoon baking powder
¼ teaspoon (or even less…) salt
⅓ cup sugar
¾ stick margarine
2 large eggs
1 teaspoon vanilla extract

Egg Wash
1 egg, beaten
1 tablespoon water

Optional ingredients
Slivered/sliced almonds, walnuts, pecans, macadamia nuts, white and dark chocolate chips (the dark chocolate 'chunks' work wonderfully), dried fruit…

Preheat oven to 350°F. Mix together dry ingredients. Cut in margarine with pastry cutter. Add eggs and vanilla. Mixture should be a little dryer than cookie dough (very crumbly). Roll out and cut into triangles. Brush tops with egg wash and sprinkle with sugar. Bake for 20 minutes or until lightly brown (don't over cook).

Pumpkin-Raisin Muffins

1 can (30-ounce) pumpkin pie mix
1 cup golden or dark raisins
½ teaspoon ground cloves
2 packages (17-ounces each) nut bread mix
1 egg, beaten
1 teaspoon cinnamon
½ teaspoon allspice

Preheat oven to 400°F. Combine all ingredients and stir until just moist. Spoon into greased tins. Sprinkle cinnamon-sugar on top of the muffins and bake for 15-20 minutes.

Soups
& Salads

Vegetable Soup

⅔ cup diced carrots
⅔ cup green beans
1 cup diced celery
1 cup diced potatoes
1 onion, diced
2 quarts meat broth (or 2 quarts boiling water plus 8 bouillon cubes)
8 tablespoons butter
2 tablespoons flour
2 cups tomatoes
Salt to taste

Prepare vegetables. Add to meat broth or boiling water and cook until vegetables are tender. Add butter. Stir flour into tomatoes. Add to cooked vegetables. Simmer about 15 minutes. Add bouillon cubes, if used, stirring until dissolved. Add salt if needed.

"This is a fairly thick soup."

James Madden, Heritage Baptist Church,
Pogue, PA

Chicken Almond Salad

1 cup cooked chicken (cut into large chunks)
½ cup celery (cut into ½-inch pieces)
1 ½ teaspoons lemon juice
Salt to taste
Pepper to taste
¼ cup mayonnaise (or yogurt)
1 or 2 hard-cooked eggs, diced
¼ cup finely broken crisp bacon (turkey bacon is great)
¼ cup chopped salted almonds

Optional serving suggestions
Tomato cups
Pineapple rings, drained
Avocado slices on salad greens

Toss chicken, celery, lemon juice, salt and pepper together. Mix in mayonnaise or yogurt. Carefully fold in eggs. Chill thoroughly. Serve in tomato cups, on drained pineapple or avocado slices on salad greens. Sprinkle with crisp bacon and salted almonds. Serves two.

"It's perfect for a summer picnic!"

Richard Boggs, Cathedral at Chapel Hill,
Decatur, GA

Strawberry Pretzel Salad

1 ½ cups pretzels, crushed
½ cup granulated sugar
½ cup melted butter
1 package (8-ounce) cream cheese, softened
1 container (8-ounce) non-dairy whipped topping
½ cup confectioners' sugar
2 small packages strawberry Jell-O®
1 cup crushed pineapple, drained
2 packages (10-ounces each) frozen strawberries.

Preheat oven to 325°F. Combine pretzels, sugar and butter. Spread in a 9x13-inch pan. Bake for 10 minutes or until light brown. Set aside to cool. Blend cream cheese, whipped topping, confectioners' sugar and spread on crushed pretzel mixture. Dissolve Jell-O® in 2 cups of boiling water. Drain pineapple. Stir drained pineapple and frozen berries into Jell-O®. Refrigerate. When slightly thickened, pour over cream cheese mixture. Keep refrigerated. Makes 12 servings.

Susan White, West Jackson Baptist Church,
Jackson, TN

Oriental Salad

1 package broccoli slaw, chopped
1 bunch green onions, chopped
½ cup oil
½ cup sugar
⅓ cup apple cider vinegar
½ cup margarine
2 packages ramen noodles, beef flavor (broken into small pieces)
¾ cup sunflower kernels
¾ cup sliced almonds

Mix broccoli slaw and green onions. Set aside. Combine oil, sugar and apple cider vinegar. Pour over slaw and onions. Refrigerate. In a medium skillet, sauté ramen noodles, sunflower kernels and almonds. Sprinkle on salad when ready to serve.

"A wonderful, crunchy salad!"

Mary McLeary, Harris Grove Methodist Church,
Humboldt, TN

Beef Stew

2 ½ pounds lean beef cubes
1 medium onion, chopped
1 cup dry red wine
½ cup consommé
3 tablespoons tomato paste
2 cloves garlic, minced
1 tablespoon olive oil
1 teaspoon salt
½ teaspoon thyme
½ teaspoon marjoram
1 pound mushrooms
4 tablespoons butter
1 package frozen peas

In a Dutch oven, brown meat and onion. Add wine, consommé, tomato paste, garlic and spices. Cover and let simmer for 2 hours or until tender. Uncover and cook down about 20 minutes. Sauté sliced mushrooms in butter. Add mushrooms and peas to stew and cook 10 minutes. Serves 6-8.

Cranberry Salad

2 packages (3-ounces each) cherry and blackberry Jell-O®
2 cups boiling water
1 pound cranberries
2 cups sugar
2 orange rinds
1 apple
1 cup crushed pineapple
1 lemon, juiced
1 cup nuts

Mix Jell-O® with water. Grind all ingredients. Let stand in sugar. Place in long Pyrex dish. Chill and serve.

Louise Peek, First Baptist Church,
Winchester, TN

Creamy Pea Salad

2 tablespoons finely chopped red onion
1 tablespoon reduced-fat mayonnaise
⅛ teaspoon salt
⅛ teaspoon pepper
½ cup frozen green peas, thawed
¼ cup diced red bell pepper
¼ cup diced cucumber

In medium bowl, combine onion, mayonnaise, salt and black pepper. Stir until well blended. Add remaining ingredients. Toss gently to coat.

Judy Heath, Cornerstone Baptist Church,
Macon, GA

Chicken-Cheese Chowder

1 cup shredded carrots
¼ cup chopped onion
4 tablespoons butter
4 tablespoons flour
2 cups milk
2 cups chicken stock
2 cups diced cooked chicken
2 tablespoons dry white wine
½ teaspoon Worcestershire sauce
½ teaspoon celery seed
Salt to taste
Freshly ground black pepper to taste
2 cups grated sharp cheddar cheese
Fresh chives, chopped

In a large saucepan, simmer carrots and onion in butter over a medium gas flame until soft but not brown. Blend in flour and cook for 1 minute, stirring constantly. Slowly pour in the milk and chicken stock and stir until thickened. Let simmer for 5 minutes. Add the cooked chicken, wine, Worcestershire sauce, and celery seed to the stock. Add salt and pepper to taste. Add the cheese and stir until just melted. Do not let it boil. Serve garnished with chopped chives. Serves 6.

Elegant Crab Soup

1 pound crab meat
4 tablespoons cognac
4 tablespoons butter
1 medium onion, finely chopped
Pepper to taste
½ teaspoon sugar
2 tablespoons flour
2 teaspoons chili seasoning
1 pint half & half

Heat crab meat and cognac, slowly in double boiler. In heavy pan melt butter, sauté onion and pepper. Mix sugar, flour and chili seasoning. Add to butter and vegetable mixture. Cook 3 minutes. Slowly stir in half & half. Fold into crab and cognac. When crab and cognac are heated, ladle into bowls. Serves 4.

Cabbage Soup

1 pound ground chuck
1 package onion soup
2 cups stewed tomatoes
1 tablespoon brown sugar
2 cups water
1 tablespoon white sugar
1 medium head of cabbage
Salt to taste
Pepper to taste

Brown meat, add all other ingredients, simmer for 2 hours. Serve with cornbread.

Note: I also substitute turkey for ground chuck and use 1 can drained kidney beans.

"It makes a great weight watchers soup!"

Summer Salad

1 squash
1 cucumber
1 small onion
1 green pepper
½ cup vinegar
¼ cup oil
½ cup water
1 teaspoon salt
Black pepper to taste
Sugar to taste
Garlic to taste

Slice squash, cucumber, onion, and green pepper. Mix vinegar, oil, water, salt, black pepper. Add sugar and garlic seasoning to taste. Pour mixture over vegetables and refrigerate until ready to serve. Keeps well for several days.

Note: You can use Italian dressing.

Mandarin Marshmallow Salad

1 box (3.4-ounce) instant vanilla pudding
2 cans (11-ounces each) mandarin oranges, undrained
1 container (8-ounce) non-dairy whipped topping, thawed
2 cups miniature marshmallows

Combine the DRY pudding mix with the undrained mandarin oranges. Mix in remaining ingredients. Refrigerate. Makes 6-8 servings.

Shirley E. Mitchell, Three Springs Assembly of God Church, Three Springs, PA

Ramen® Noodles Salad

<u>Dressing</u>
¾ cup oil
½ cup sugar
⅓ cup white vinegar
2 packages Ramen® seasoning (comes in the package with noodles.)

<u>Salad</u>
2 packages Ramen® noodles, chicken flavored
1 package (16-ounce) cabbage slaw mix, finely chopped
2 bunches of green onions, chopped
1 cup sliced almonds
1 cup sunflower kernels

Assemble first 4 ingredients in a medium saucepan. Heat to melt sugar. Let stand to room temperature. Place the next 5 ingredients in a large bowl. Do not cook Ramen® Noodles. Break into smaller pieces, if desired. Add the room temperature dressing 1-2 hours before serving time.

Gail Chandler, Sulphur Well Church of Christ, Springville, TN

Raw Vegetable Salad

4 cups shredded cabbage
1 teaspoon celery seed
2 cucumbers cut in small bits
½ teaspoon white pepper
1 cup sugar
2 cups white vinegar
2 green peppers, chopped
1 teaspoon celery salt
4 shredded carrots
1 teaspoon onion salt
2 teaspoons salt

Mix well. Throw in piece of ice to crisp all ingredients. Delicious for luncheon or dinner.

Cabbage Salad

½ small head of cabbage, shredded
1 – 1 ½ cups of carrots, shredded
½ cup + 1 teaspoon olive oil
1 package Ramen® noodles (omit seasoning packet)
¼ cup sliced almonds
2 tablespoons sesame seeds
3 green onions, chopped
⅓ cup apple cider vinegar
¼ cup sugar
1 teaspoon soy sauce

Chop cabbage and carrots using salad shooter and mix together in bowl. Put about a teaspoon of olive oil in a skillet, crush Ramen® Noodles and add to oil stirring to blend. Add almonds and let set for a few minutes. Toast noodles and almonds for a few minutes in the teaspoon of olive oil, stirring to avoid burning. Add sesame seeds and continue to stir while toasting. Remove from heat and allow to cool slightly. Mix all remaining ingredients together and blend with a whisk until well mixed.

Note: This salad will keep for several days; however, don't put the toasted mixture on the veggies or put salad dressing on the veggies until you are ready to serve. The moisture will make the noodles soft and the dressing will wilt the veggies. This is great with barbeque or grilled foods, or just by itself with fresh bread.

Irish Potato Salad

6 cups cold potatoes, cut in small pieces

2 teaspoons celery salt

1 teaspoon celery seed

3 hard-boiled eggs, chopped fine

3 green peppers, cut fine

1 can pimentos, cut in bits

½ cup chopped sweet pickle

3 onions, minced

1 teaspoon white or black pepper

Dash of cayenne pepper

Dash of paprika

1 ½ pints mustard

1 quart mayonnaise

Mix all ingredients well. Chill and serve. Best ever.

4-H Special

1 cup rice, uncooked
2 quarts boiling water
2 teaspoons salt
1 onion
2 cups hamburger
2 tablespoons solid shortening
1 ½ cups tomatoes
2 cups canned corn

Preheat oven to 350°F. Cook rice in boiling salted water until tender. Drain. Run hot water over rice and drain again. Cook onion and meat in 2 tablespoons fat until well done. Combine all ingredients. Put in greased casserole and bake for 20 minutes.

Note: Corn may be omitted if an extra ½ cup of uncooked rice and ½ cup of meat are added.

Helen Madden, Heritage Baptist Church,
Pogue, PA

Raw Cranberry Salad

1 package (12-ounce) cranberries
1 orange, whole
1 red apple, whole
Nuts (optional)
1 box (3-ounce) cherry Jell-O®
1 cup sugar

Grind together the cranberries, orange, apple and nuts. Leave peeling on the fruit. Make the Jell-O® according to directions. Before it chills, combine sugar and ground fruits with Jell-O®. Chill and serve. This salad will keep for quite some time in the refrigerator.

Old Fashioned Slaw

3 cups shredded cabbage, do not shred fine
2 cucumbers, cut in small pieces
2 large carrots, shredded
3 green peppers
1 tablespoon salt
1 quart white vinegar
2 cups sugar
1 tablespoon celery seed
1 teaspoon white pepper

Mix thoroughly. Thirty minutes before serving put in a small handful of crushed ice. Ice makes salad crisp and dilutes vinegar. You can use the same ingredients for frozen slaw but substitute 1 quart mayonnaise instead of vinegar. Place in refrigerator to chill. Serve with cheese wafers.

Spinach Salad

6 cups washed chopped spinach
¼ cup celery, cut up
1 red or green onion
4 eggs, sliced
½ teaspoon salt
Pepper to taste
1 package garlic cheese salad dressing
3 tablespoons lemon juice
1 cup sour cream

Combine spinach, celery, onion, eggs, salt and pepper. Set in refrigerator several hours. When ready to serve combine with other ingredients.

Granny's Green Jell-O® Salad

1 ¼ pounds marshmallows
1 cup milk
1 large package lime Jell-O®
6 ounces cream cheese
1 can (20-ounce) crushed pineapple
1 cup pecans, chopped
1 container (8-ounce) non-dairy whipped topping

Melt marshmallows and milk in top of a double boiler. Remove from heat and add lime Jell-O®. Stir in, until completely dissolved. Let cool if necessary (so the cream cheese won't curdle) then add 6-ounces cream cheese. Whisk until smooth. Add crushed pineapple. Stir in pecans. Fold in whipped topping. Spread in 13x9-inch dish. Chill until firm.

Meats

Breakfast Squares

2 cans crescent rolls
1 pound hot sausage
8 slices cheese

Preheat oven to 325°F. Brown meat. Drain off excess fat. Place
1 can of crescent rolls on cookie sheet. Put cooked meat in then
the slices of cheese on top. Put second can on top. Pull to cover
the top. Bake for 15-20 minutes until golden brown. Let cool.
Then cut into squares.

Jill Peek, Brentwood Baptist Church,
Brentwood, TN

Pecan-Coated Fried Crappie

2 eggs, beaten
½ teaspoon salt
¼ teaspoon pepper
1 cup unseasoned dry bread crumbs
1 cup ground pecans
8 fillets
Peanut oil

In a mixing bowl, combine eggs, salt and pepper. In another bowl, combine bread crumbs and pecans. Pour bread crumb mixture onto a plate. Dip fillets in egg mixture, then roll in crumbs to coat. Add to the crumbs on the plate as needed. In a skillet, heat ¼-inch oil to 350°F–375°F. Add fillets, fry fillets for 3 minutes, turning once.

John Shelton, Bells, TN

Sausage Jambalaya

1 pound smoked sausage, sliced
1 onion, diced
1 pepper, diced
2 cloves garlic, minced
2 ¼ cups chicken broth
1 ½ cups converted rice
1 can diced tomatoes, drained
1 cup kernel corn, drained
1 tablespoon Cajun seasoning

Sauté the sausage, onion, peppers and garlic in large skillet. Stir in all other ingredients and bring to a boil. Reduce heat. Stir, cover and simmer for 25 minutes.

Larry & Brenda Wisse, Trinity Lutheran Church,
Marysville, OH

Chinese Chicken

2 cups cooked chicken, cubed/diced
1 cup rice, cooked
1 cup fresh mushroom, sliced/diced
1 can cream of chicken soup
1 can (4-ounce) water chestnuts, drained and slivered
1 cup celery, chopped
1 teaspoon lemon juice
1 teaspoon salt
1 tablespoon onion flakes (or use fresh chopped onion)
¾ cup mayonnaise
1 cup butter cracker crumbs
½ cup butter
½ cup slivered almonds

Preheat oven to 350°F. Mix all ingredients together, except cracker crumbs, butter, and almonds. Put mixture in 2-quart casserole dish. Melt cracker crumbs, butter, and slivered almonds. Top casserole with cracker mixture, and bake for 35 minutes or until brown on top.

Dottie Moore, Inglewood Baptist Church,
Nashville, TN

Dutch Meatloaf

1 ½ pounds ground beef
1 medium onion
1 ½ teaspoons salt
¾ cup water
2 tablespoons prepared mustard
1 egg
¼ teaspoon pepper
2 tablespoons brown sugar
1 tablespoon vinegar
¾ cups oatmeal (or 1 cup of bread crumbs)
4 ounces tomato sauce (or 6-ounces salsa)

Preheat oven to 350°F. Mix the ingredients well and put in a baking pan (preferably one that drains the grease below the loaf). Spread tomato sauce on top. Bake for 1 hour.

Glen Taylor, Fellowship Brethren Church,
Garrison, IA

Chicken Enchilada Bake

2 cups diced cooked chicken
½ pound pasteurized process cheese spread, cubed
1 can (16-ounce) pinto beans
1 can (2 ¼-ounce) sliced ripe olives, drained
½ cup salsa
1 tablespoon chili powder
¼ teaspoon garlic powder
1 cup baking mix
¾ cup milk
2 tablespoons melted butter or margarine

Preheat oven to 425°F. Grease a 2-quart baking dish. Combine chicken, cheese, beans, olives, salsa, chili powder and garlic powder in large mixing bowl; blend well. Spoon into prepared dish; set aside. To prepare crust, combine baking mix, milk and butter in mixing bowl; blend well. Pour over chicken mixture. Bake 30-35 minutes or until crust is golden brown. Serves 6-8.

Chili Dog Pie

2 ½ cups baking mix
3 tablespoons prepared yellow mustard
6 tablespoons water
1 package (16-ounce) hot dogs
2 cans (15-ounces each) chili (or 4 cups homemade chili)
½ cup shredded cheddar cheese

Preheat oven to 425°F. Grease a 13x9x2-inch baking dish. Combine baking mix, mustard and water in small mixing bowl. Stir until dough forms. With fingertips dipped in baking mix, press dough into bottom and up sides of prepared dish; set aside. Quarter hot dogs by cutting in half lengthwise and again crosswise. Place hot dogs on dough. Spread chili over hot dogs. Sprinkle with cheese. Bake 20 minutes or until heated through. Serves 6-8.

Gorgonzola & Mushroom Stuffed Beef Tenderloin with Merlot Sauce

<u>Beef</u>
1 beef tenderloin (about 2 ½ pounds)
1 tablespoon butter
1 cup sliced fresh mushrooms
1 cup soft breadcrumbs
½ cup crumbled Gorgonzola cheese
¼ cup chopped fresh parsley
1 tablespoon olive oil
¼ teaspoon salt

<u>Merlot Sauce</u>
½ cup currant jelly
½ cup merlot, zinfandel or non-alcoholic red wine
¼ cup beef broth
1 tablespoon butter

Heat oven to 425°F. Cut beef horizontally down length of meat, about ½-inch from the top of beef to within ½-inch of opposite side; open flat. Turn beef. Repeat with other side of beef, cutting from the inside edge to within ½-inch of opposite edge; open flat.

In 10-inch skillet, melt butter over medium-high heat. Cook mushrooms in butter until tender and liquid has evaporated. Cool 5 minutes. Add breadcrumbs, cheese, and parsley; toss to combine.

Sprinkle breadcrumb mixture over beef to within 1 inch of edges. Tightly roll up beef, beginning with long side. Turn small end of beef under about 6 inches so it cooks evenly. Tie beef with butcher's string at about 1 ½-inch intervals. In shallow roasting pan, place beef, seam side down on rack. Brush with oil; sprinkle with salt. Insert meat thermometer so tip is in center of thickest part of beef. Bake uncovered 30-40 minutes or until thermometer reads at least 140°F. Cover loosely with foil and let stand 15 minutes or until thermometer reads 145°F.

Meanwhile, in 1-quart saucepan, heat all sauce ingredients to boiling stirring occasionally. Reduce heat to low. Simmer uncovered 35-40 minutes, stirring occasionally, until sauce is slightly reduced and syrupy. Remove string from beef before carving. Serve beef with sauce.

Mary Beth Pederson, Illinois State Fair,
Springfield, IL

Chicken Pot Pie With Butter Crust

5 pounds skinless meaty chicken pieces
6 cups water (or chicken broth)
1 large onion, quartered
1 tablespoon salt plus ½ teaspoon
2 ½ cups potatoes, cubed
1 ½ cups onions, finely chopped
4 medium carrots (strips)
1 cup celery
2 ⅔ cups all-purpose flour
4 teaspoons baking powder
½ teaspoon pepper
1 egg, beaten
1 cup milk
3 tablespoons butter, melted

Preheat oven to 450°F. In Dutch oven or large pan, combine chicken and water (or chicken broth), onion and 1 tablespoon salt. Bring to a boil and reduce heat, cover and simmer 40 minutes or until tender. Remove chicken from broth, save broth, cool chicken. Remove meat from bone and cut in small pieces. (You can use boneless chicken if you want.)

In another pan, cook potatoes, onions, carrots, and celery, covered in small amount of boiling water for 10 minutes or until tender. Drain, divide chicken and vegetables into two ungreased 2-quart casseroles.

For gravy: Skim fat from broth and discard. Reserve 4 cups of broth. Return broth to Dutch oven and heat through. Stir together 1 cup water and ⅔ cup flour and ½ teaspoon of pepper. Add to broth, cook and stir until thick and bubbly. Remove from heat, cover and keep warm.

For crust: In large mixing bowl, stir together remaining 2 cups flour, baking powder and ½ teaspoon salt. In medium bowl combine egg, milk, melted butter, stir just until moistened. Divide the warm gravy between the two casseroles. Drop dough in small rounds on top of gravy. Bake casseroles immediately in oven for 10 minutes or reduce heat to 400°F and bake 8-10 minutes or until golden brown. Serve warm. (Do not freeze.) Serves 4-5 per casserole. For small gathering cut recipe in half.

5-Minute Crock Pot Burritos

3 pounds sirloin end pork roast
2 teaspoons southwest seasoning
3 cups salsa (2 cups plus 1 cup)
6-8 tortillas
1 cup grated cheese
Diced fresh cilantro

Rub pork roast with southwest seasoning and place in crockpot. Pour 2 cups salsa over roast and cook on low 6-8 hours. When the meat falls off the bone, shred with a fork. Heat tortillas and fill with meat mixture. Arrange on platter and top with remaining salsa and cheese. Put under the broiler until cheese is bubbly. Garnish with cilantro. Serve on a bed of black beans or Spanish rice. Serves 4-6.

Renae Woods, Utah State Fair,
Salt Lake City, UT

Coca-Cola® Roast

1 roast (2 ½ pounds)
1 bottle (16-ounce) Coca-Cola®
1 envelope onion soup mix
1 can mushroom soup
Potatoes and carrots, optional

Preheat oven to 325°F. Place a roast in a roaster (or crock pot). Pour ½ bottle of Coca-Cola® over the roast. Sprinkle onion soup mix over Coke®. Then spread mushroom soup over roast. Pour rest of Coca-Cola® over top of roast. Bake for 1 hour or until internal thermometer inserted in the thickest part reaches 170°F.

Alice Taylor, Fellowship Brethren Church,
Garrison, IA

Delicious Pork Chops

6 pork chops
2 eggs
Salt to taste
Cracker meal

Select 6 well trimmed chops. Beat 2 eggs. Salt chops. Dip chops in beaten eggs, then in cracker meal. Dip in the eggs again and the cracker meal. Put in vessel with hot oil and brown. Served with sliced pineapple that has been dipped in brown sugar and cooked in butter until brown.

Chicken Puffs

1 package (8-ounce) cream cheese, softened
1 medium onion
1 cup cooked rice
4 chicken breasts
3 packages of crescent rolls

Topping
1 can cream of chicken soup
Milk
1 can English peas, drained (or asparagus, cut into bite size pieces)

For puffs: Preheat oven to 350°F. Boil chicken. Pick off bone and chop. Cook rice as per instructions on box. Mince onion. Mix all ingredients together. Seam crescent rolls into a square roll. Place in 2 tablespoons of the mixture in the middle of the pastry square. Pinch pastry together. Bake for 10-12 minutes. The square roll can be cut in half, to make two small puffs instead of one large one, if desired.

For topping: Empty contents of a chicken soup can into a small bowl. Add milk to desired consistency. Add drained peas or cut asparagus. Spoon over individual puffs. Serve immediately.

Joanne Goldstein, Jackson, TN

Fruited Flank Steak

1-1 ½ pounds flank steak
Salt to taste
Pepper to taste
1 can (30-ounce) fruit cocktail
1 teaspoon vinegar
1 tablespoon salad oil
1 clove garlic, minced
1 tablespoon lemon juice
¼ cup teriyaki sauce

Sprinkle flank steak with salt and pepper; place in slow cooker. Drain fruit cocktail, saving ¼ cup syrup. Combine ¼ cup syrup with remaining ingredients; pour over steak in cooker. Cover and cook on low for 7-9 hours or until tender. Add drained fruit the last few minutes. Lift out of pot; place on platter. Serves 4-5.

Fried Chicken

(Southern Style)

1 fat (2 ½ pound) young chicken
1 cup flour
½ teaspoon salt
¼ teaspoon black pepper

Gravy
1 tablespoon flour
1 cup cream
Salt to taste

For chicken: Cut in ten pieces. Separate the legs and thighs. (Do not have part of back on any of the pieces.) Wash thoroughly. Dredge chicken in flour that is mixed with salt and pepper. Place in an iron skillet of deep, hot fat and cook for 25 minutes. Do not cover. Let cook until a golden brown.

For chicken gravy: Half of the strained fat, used in the frying with 1 tablespoon of flour and 1 cup of cream. Pinch of salt.

Spamtacular Sunnydogs

1 can (12-ounce) original Spam®
1 ½ cups pancake batter
2 eggs
½ cup applesauce
1 teaspoon vanilla
⅛ teaspoon cinnamon
¼ cup water
18 toothpicks

Cut Spam® widthwise into 6 sections (½-inch pieces). Then cut the sections into thirds (½-inch pieces makes 18 pieces). Put toothpick halfway in one end of Spam®. Mix pancake batter, eggs, applesauce, cinnamon, and vanilla together in a bowl. Add water slowly until batter is thick. Use toothpick to dip Spam® into batter and then place in non-stick pan. Cook until bottom is light brown. Use toothpick to turn over and finish cooking other side to brown. Dip into honey, syrup, or applesauce and eat.

Cynthia Coombs, Utah State Fair, Salt Lake City, UT

Chicken Stir-Fry

¼ cup orange juice
1 ½ tablespoons cornstarch
1 pound skinless, boneless chicken breasts, cut into strips
¾ cup chicken broth
1 ½ tablespoons soy sauce
2 ½ teaspoons vegetable oil
1 clove garlic, minced
1 tablespoon minced fresh ginger or 1 ½ teaspoon ground ginger
1 ½ cups snow peas or green beans
1 medium red bell pepper, cut into thin strips (about 1 cup)
¾ cup sliced green onion
1 cup frozen broccoli, thawed
1 medium carrot, thinly sliced
2 cups cooked white rice

In a shallow glass bowl, combine orange juice and cornstarch; mix well. Stir in chicken. Cover and chill for 2 hours. Drain chicken; discard juice mixture. In a small bowl, combine broth and soy sauce. Set aside. In a wok or large nonstick skillet, heat oil over medium heat. Add garlic and ginger; stir-fry for 30 seconds. Add chicken; stir-fry for 3 minutes. Add vegetables; stir-fry until crisp-tender, about 5 minutes. Stir in broth mixture. Place ½ cup of rice on each serving plate. Top with the chicken mixture, dividing evenly.

Crusty Lamb Chops

1 tablespoon mayonnaise
2 tablespoons spicy brown mustard
⅛ cup oil
1 tablespoon sour cream
⅛ teaspoon crushed dried rosemary leaves
1 dash ground cloves
1 dash garlic powder
1 dash onion salt
1 slice bread, torn into pieces
½ cup ground pecans
¼ teaspoon freshly ground pepper
1 pound lamb blade chops

Preheat oven to 350°F. Mix mayonnaise, mustard and oil in a small bowl. Place remaining ingredients into blender. Use pulse setting to mix thoroughly. Brush mustard mixture onto each chop. Coat in crumb mixture. Place in a greased baking pan. Cook 35-45 minutes or until done. Serves 4.

Jeanine Mower Anderson, Utah State Fair, Salt Lake City, UT

Tri Tip Roast

1 tri tip roast (2-3 pounds) with Santa Maria Marinade®
1 pound baby red potatoes
6 ears of corn, cut in cobbett
1 container (8-ounce) mushroom caps

Grease a Dutch oven with olive oil. Preheat to 300°F. Take roast out of marinade. Set marinade aside. Pat dry. Lightly dust roast with flour and brown in Dutch oven. Place in preheated Dutch oven. Roast (low propane on bottom and 12 coals on top) for 1 ½ - 2 hours or until internal temperature reaches 145°F-150°F. When roast has cooked for 1 hour place corn and potatoes in a pan. Add remaining marinade. Bring to a boil. Take roast out of Dutch oven. Place corn and potatoes in bottom. Take roasting shelf and place on top of the vegetables. Return roast to oven, then add mushrooms. Baste roast with remaining vegetable liquid. Continue to cook until done.

Dana Hancock & David Jones, Utah State Fair,
Salt Lake City, UT

Roast Rib of Beef Au Jus and Horseradish Cream

<u>Roast Rib of Beef</u>
6-7 pounds beef rib roast
2 tablespoons minced onions
2 tablespoons whole peppercorns
2 tablespoons gourmet sea salt coarse grind
2 tablespoons dry sage
2 tablespoons granulated garlic
1 tablespoon paprika
1 tablespoon dried thyme
1 tablespoon marjoram
2 tablespoons flour
1 large onion, sliced
1 cup whiskey or beef broth

<u>Horseradish Cream</u>
¾ cup heavy cream (whipping cream)
½ cup mayonnaise
¼ cup prepared horseradish
1 tablespoon Dijon mustard
Pinch of sugar

Reserve ribs from roast. Grind the minced onions, peppercorns, sea salt, and dry spices. Rub this into the outside surface of the meat. If you run out of the spices mixture make more and keep at it until the whole thing is covered. Preheat Dutch oven over medium heat for 10 minutes. Trim excess fat from the roast. Place 2-3 rib bones on the bottom of Dutch oven. Arrange the roast on top of the rib bones. Add sliced onions and the whiskey or beef broth. Once the meat is done to your preference, remove from oven and let it stand for 15-20 minutes before slicing. If you have to change coals, do it every 45 minutes.

For gravy: Reserve pan drippings for gravy. Add flour mix well with the juice. Bring to a boil and let simmer until thickened. Strain juices through a coarse sieve. Serve gravy in a 5-inch Dutch oven.

For horseradish cream: Salt and freshly ground pepper to taste. Whip the cream in a bowl until it forms soft peaks. In a separate bowl combine the mayonnaise, horseradish and mustard. Using a rubber spatula, fold in the whipped cream. Add sugar, salt and pepper. Stir well and transfer into bell pepper or tomatoes.

Rosa and Marisela Sanchez, Utah State Fair, Salt Lake City, UT

Chili Chili, Bang Bang!

<u>Part 1</u>
3 pounds beef chuck tender, cubed
1-2 tablespoons olive oil
6-8 cloves garlic, minced
2 cans (14 ½-ounces each) cans beef broth
2 cans (14 ½-ounces each) tomato puree
4 dashes hot sauce (or to taste)
1 ½ tablespoons onion powder
¾ teaspoon red pepper (cayenne)
2 teaspoons beef bouillon granules
1 teaspoon chicken bouillon granules

<u>Part 2</u>
¾ teaspoon garlic powder
1 ½ tablespoons cumin
¾ teaspoon white pepper
6 tablespoons chili powder
Salt to taste

Brown meat in olive oil and garlic. Cover with 2 cans of beef broth. Stir in ½ of the tomato puree, all the hot sauce, and all the other ingredients of Part 1. Cook on medium; boil until the meat is tender. Add water or broth as needed. Thirty minutes before serving, add the ingredients of Part 2 and simmer to smooth, even consistency.

Ben & Kim Watson, Utah State Fair,
Salt Lake City, UT

Chardonnay Pork

<u>Pork Tenderloin</u>
1 pound pork tenderloin slices (3 or 4, ½-inch thick)
1 cup sliced fresh mushrooms (or small can)
⅔ cup chardonnay
10 ounces water or fat free canned chicken broth
1 cup sour cream
1-2 tablespoons flour
Salt and pepper to taste

<u>Marinade</u>
⅓ cup water or broth
⅓ cup wine
⅓ cup oil
½ teaspoon minced garlic (1 clove)
Fresh herbs: 2-3 sage leaves, 6-8 basil leaves, 2 teaspoons rosemary,
2 teaspoons chopped chives
If dried herbs are used: ¼ teaspoon sage, 1 teaspoon basil, ½ teaspoon
rosemary, ½ teaspoon chives

Pierce tenderloin slices with fork, several times on both sides. Place in zippered plastic bag with marinade. Refrigerate for several hours or overnight. When ready to cook, sauté mushrooms in 2 teaspoons butter, margarine or oil. Remove to dish. Drain meat and discard marinade. Brown tenderloin slices in mushroom pan. Season with salt and pepper or paprika. Add ½ cup liquid, ⅓ cup wine, 1-2 chopped green onions and mushrooms. Reduce heat to simmer, cover and cook gently 45 minutes (may also be placed in 325°F oven.) Remove meat to warm dish. Add flour to remaining liquid and thicken. (If needed, add additional liquid.) Salt and pepper to taste. Add sour cream and heat through. Pour over pork tenderloin slices and serve hot.

"I serve this dish over egg noodles with whole fresh green beans. Garnish with fresh herbs for eye appeal."

Natalie (Mickey) Williams, Michigan State Fair, Detroit, MI

PennyWise Skillet Supper Dish

1 tablespoon butter or margarine
4 frankfurters
1 medium onion
¼ cup water
½ cup catsup
1 tablespoon prepared mustard
1 teaspoon vinegar
1 can (1 pound 10-ounce) pork & beans in tomato sauce
1 can (8-ounce) kidney beans, drained

In skillet heat butter or margarine and sauté onions. Brown sliced frankfurters. Stir in remaining ingredients. Simmer in covered skillet for 30 minutes. Makes 4-6 servings.

Helen Madden, Heritage Baptist Church,
Pogue, PA

Meatballs Royale

2 pounds frozen meatballs (Italian style)
1 can (16-ounce) jellied cranberry sauce
2 tablespoons brown sugar
1 tablespoon lemon juice
1 bottle (12-ounce) chili sauce

Simmer all ingredients until the cranberry sauce melts. Can be served over rice or baked potatoes.

Susan White, West Jackson Baptist Church,
Jackson, TN

Chili Chili

1 pound ground chuck (browned and drained)
¼ cup chili powder
3 heaping tablespoons cumin
1 can tomatoes
3 cans chili beans
1 can tomato sauce

In large pot combine ground chuck with the chili powder, cumin, tomatoes, chili beans and tomato sauce. Simmer until done.

Gail Chandler, Sulphur Well Church of Christ,
Springville, TN

Bar-B-Que

1 large pork shoulder
Whole pecans, shelled
1 can (10-ounce) frozen orange juice concentrate, thawed
2 tablespoons lemon juice concentrate
15 ounces water
15 ounces white vinegar
½ tablespoon cayenne pepper
1 tablespoon lemon pepper
1 teaspoon garlic salt
2 teaspoons prepared dry mustard or ¼ cup yellow salad mustard

Build a low fire and crack open the top and bottom grill vents to less than ¼-inch. While keeping the meat away from the direct heat, place unshelled pecans over direct heat. (The smoke from the roasting pecans will flavor the meat.) Slow roast pork shoulder to 170°F internal temperature (5-7 hours). Place remaining ingredients in a 2-quart jar. Use mixture as a roasting baste and as a sauce when eating.

Dakota County Fair, Farmington, MN

Savory Sausage Shells

1 package mild sausage
1 ½ cups of frozen onion and ½ cup three pepper combination, sautéed
2 cups of sautéed mushrooms
1 container cream cheese (chive and onion flavor)
1 package (3-ounce) cream cheese
1 container (15-ounce) ricotta cheese
1 cup of shredded mozzarella cheese
1 package frozen spinach
1 package jumbo pasta shells
2 jars spaghetti sauce (robust flavor/roasted garlic)
1 can diced tomatoes with basil/onion/pepper
Dried tomatoes, optional

Preheat oven to 350°F. Brown sausage with ½ cup of onions and peppers and set aside. Prepare pasta shells according to directions on package. Allow them to cool. (They will be easier to fill without tearing.) Refrigerate shortly. Sauté the mushrooms and the remaining 1 ½ cups of onions/peppers and set aside. Mix together the cream cheeses, the ricotta cheese, and 2 cups of mozzarella cheese.

To the cheese mixture, add half of the sausage combination and mix again. Next mix in half of the spinach (which has been cooked in the microwave). Mix together the cheeses, sausage combination, and spinach. Spoon the mixture into the pasta shells and set aside. In separate bowl, combine 2 jars of spaghetti sauce, can of diced tomatoes, and the remaining sausage, mushrooms, peppers, onions, and spinach. Spoon some of the sauce mixture into the bottom of a large rectangular glass dish. Next, put the stuffed shells into 2 rows in the glass dish. Cover with the sauce mixture remaining. Bake in oven for 30-35 minutes. Take out dish and add mozzarella, more peppers and mushrooms (if desired). Add dried tomatoes and/or any other toppings your taste buds enjoy. Put back into the oven for 5 minutes to melt.

Tricia Satkowski, Arkansas State Fair,
Little Rock, AR

Beef Tips

1 package beef tips
1 teaspoon Nature's Seasoning®
2 cups water
3 large potatoes
1 large package frozen vegetables
1 large can stewed tomatoes
1 small onion, diced

Spray skillet with non-stick cooking spray. Sauté beef tips in skillet, sprinkle with Nature's Seasoning®. Cook until brown on all sides. Move to large pot, and add water, bring to rolling boil. Cut potatoes into small cubes. Add potatoes and frozen vegetables. Cook for 10 minutes then reduce heat to simmer. Add tomatoes, onion and 1 teaspoon of Nature's Seasoning®. Cook for 10 more minutes or until vegetables are soft.

Lisa Hays, Daystar International Church,
Mt. Olive, AL

Cajun Grilled Chicken

4 boneless skinless chicken breast halves
2 tablespoons lemon juice
2 tablespoons paprika
3 tablespoons Mrs. Dash Extra Spicy Seasoning®
1 tablespoon brown sugar
Cooking spray

Preheat grill to medium-high. Slash each piece of chicken in 2-3 places with ¼-inch deep cuts. In bowl, combine chicken and lemon juice, turning the chicken until it is thoroughly coated. Set aside. In separate bowl, mix Mrs. Dash®, paprika and brown sugar. Take each piece of chicken and roll in the spice mixture until well coated. Spray grill with cooking spray and place seasoned chicken breasts on the grill. Cook 5 minutes on each side or until juices run clear when a skewer is inserted. Serve immediately.

Judy Heath, Cornerstone Baptist Church,
Macon, GA

Vegetables

Baked Tomato Wedges

2 tablespoons fine dry bread crumbs
¼ cup finely chopped onion
¼ cup fresh parsley
½ clove garlic, minced
2 tablespoons margarine, melted
½ teaspoon salt
⅛ teaspoon pepper
¼ teaspoon basil
4 tomatoes

Preheat oven to 425°F. Mix first 8 ingredients in a bowl. Cut each tomato into 8 wedges. Place in greased 7x11-inch casserole. Sprinkle tomato wedges with bread crumb mixture. Bake for 8 minutes. Serves 4.

Baked Beans

1 ½ pounds ground beef
½ medium green pepper, diced
1 medium onion, diced
Dash of hot sauce
1 teaspoon chili powder
Salt to taste
Pepper to taste
3 cans (28-ounces each) baked beans
1 bottle chili sauce

Preheat oven to 350°F. Brown ground beef, drain. Add green pepper, onion, hot sauce, chili powder, salt and pepper. Cook 5 minutes. Place beans in 6 quart ovenproof casserole dish. Add ground beef mixture and bottle of chili sauce. Mix well. Bake uncovered for 45-60 minutes.

Shirley M. Meredith, Sacred Heart Church, Conemaugh, PA

German Potato Salad

1 cup water
½ cup vinegar
2 tablespoons flour
2 tablespoons bacon drippings
⅔ cup sugar (more if desired)
1 teaspoon salt
⅛ teaspoon pepper
1 quart cooked potatoes, sliced or diced
1 medium onion, chopped
4-6 strips bacon, fried and crumbled

Combine water, vinegar, and flour in saucepan. Cook, stirring constantly, until thick. Add bacon drippings, sugar, salt, and pepper; mix thoroughly. Pour sauce over cooked potatoes, onions and bacon. Let set about 20 minutes to absorb flavors before serving.

Roy Simmons, First Lutheran Church,
Neosho, MO

Sweet Potato Pudding

5 cups coarsely grated, raw sweet potatoes
¾ cup brown sugar
½ cup sugar
1 ½ cups half & half
½ cup melted butter
3 eggs, well beaten
½ teaspoon each – nutmeg, cinnamon, allspice, cloves
1 teaspoon vanilla
½ cup seedless raisins
½ cup chopped toasted pecans
Whipped cream or ice cream
Caramel sauce, optional

Preheat oven to 400°F. Mix all ingredients and pour into a buttered casserole dish. Bake for 50-60 minutes. As the crust begins to form around the edges, remove from oven and stir throughout. Do this several times until baking is finished. Serve warm topped with whipped cream or ice cream. Yummy with a little of your favorite caramel sauce drizzled across the top.

"I remember my mother, Carrie Brewer, making this for church suppers over sixty years ago."

Josephine Murphy, 1st Methodist Church, Jackson, TN

Vegetarian Baked Beans

2 cans (30-ounces each) pork and beans
2 cans (30-ounces each) red kidney beans
2 medium onions, chopped fine
1 cup brown sugar, lightly packed
1 cup barbeque sauce
¼ cup honey mustard
½ cup chopped pecans
½ cup molasses

Preheat oven to 350°F. Put beans into large baking dish. Add chopped onions, brown sugar, barbeque sauce, honey mustard, and molasses and mix well. Sprinkle chopped pecans over top. Bake for 1 hour.

"We have always served the milk gravy on toast with fried potatoes and applesauce. Other families serve it over biscuits with mashed potatoes. Right before everyone sits down at the table, fry up lots of extra tomatoes to serve on the side. Although I lost my father over 10 years ago, I will never forget how happy this meal would always make him. His face would light up like a little child as we sat down at the table. It is cherished moments like this that I will carry in my heart forever."

John Elbirn,
Bridgeton, NJ

Broccoli Casserole

½ pound processed cheese spread
2 packages frozen chopped broccoli, cooked and drained
½ pound Ritz® crackers
½ stick margarine

Preheat oven to 350°F. Cut cheese to melt easily. Mix with broccoli and pour into buttered casserole dish. Crush crackers (1 roll) with rolling pin. Mix with margarine and sprinkle on top of broccoli mixture. Bake 20-30 minutes.

Tomato Supreme

6 large, ripe tomatoes
¼ teaspoon salt
1 medium green pepper, chopped
1 medium onion, chopped
1 crushed garlic clove
1 egg, beaten well
1 cup cooked white rice
¼ cup melted butter
1 cup cheddar cheese, shredded
¼ cup parmesan cheese

Preheat oven to 350°F. Cut the top from each tomato, scoop out the pulp. Be careful to leave the shell intact. Sprinkle inside shell lightly with salt; turn over to drain. Chop tomato pulp. Sauté green pepper, onion and garlic in butter, add tomato pulp and remaining ingredients, mix well. Spoon mixture into shells. Place in shallow baking dish. Bake for 20 minutes. Take out and sprinkle with parmesan cheese and herbed pepper according to taste. Return to oven for 10 more minutes. Serves 6.

Buttery Crunch Topped Tomatoes

2 tablespoons butter, melted
⅓ cup coarsely crushed buttery crackers
½ cup (2-ounce) cheddar cheese, shredded
2 tablespoons butter
¼ teaspoon salt
⅛ teaspoon pepper
1 tablespoon chopped onion
2 large ripe tomatoes, cut into 10-12 wedges

In small bowl stir together melted butter, crackers and cheese, set aside. In skillet melt butter, stir in salt and pepper and onion (optional). Add tomatoes. Cover; cook over medium heat stirring occasionally, until tomatoes are heated through (2-3 minutes). Sprinkle with cheese mixture, cover let stand for 1 minute. Serve immediately.

Copper Pennies

2 pounds fresh carrots
2 medium onions
1 medium green pepper
⅔ cup sugar
¾ cup vinegar
½ teaspoon salt
1 teaspoon prepared mustard
½ cup cooking oil
1 can (10 ¾-ounce) tomato soup
1 teaspoon Worcestershire sauce

Slice carrots into ¼-inch rounds (4 ½ cups). Thinly slice and separate the onions into rings. Slice the green pepper. Cook the carrots in a small amount of boiling salted water until just tender (8-10 minutes). Drain and combine with onion and green pepper in large bowl. Combine remaining ingredients in a separate mixing bowl. Pour over vegetables. Cover and marinate in the refrigerator overnight. Drain before serving.

Cabbage Stew

½ head cabbage, shredded
2 large onions, slice & ring
½ cup water
1 pound hamburger
1 quart tomato juice
2 cans (16-ounce) kidney beans
1 teaspoon chili powder
Salt to taste
Pepper to taste

Place onion and cabbage in old iron pot. Add water. Cook until yellow. Brown hamburger. Pour off fat. Add all ingredients to hamburger and cook until done (about 30 minutes).

"You don't have to use an old iron pot but it's fun to make it in one."

Zucchini Bake

3 cups thinly sliced zucchini
½ cup sliced green onion
2 tablespoons chopped parsley
Dash hot sauce or cayenne pepper
½ cup vegetable oil
1 cup buttermilk biscuit mix
½ cup Parmesan cheese grated
½ teaspoon Italian seasoning
¼ teaspoon garlic powder
4 eggs, slightly beaten

Preheat oven to 350°F. Grease shallow glass baking dish. Mix all ingredients together and pour in baking dish. Bake for 25 minutes or until golden brown. Cool 5 minutes and cut into squares.

Corn Sauté

6-8 large to medium ears of fresh corn
½ cup finely chopped green onions
3 tablespoons butter
½ teaspoon herbed pepper
¼ cup water
Salt to taste

Shuck corn. Cut from cob with a sharp knife then scrape juice from cob. Add green onions. Sauté corn and onions in butter over low heat until tender. If necessary, add a small amount of water. Salt to taste. Serve while hot.

Delicious Stuffed Squash

12 squash (gourd variety)
6 tablespoons melted butter
½ teaspoon sugar
⅛ teaspoon black pepper
6 tablespoons butter
2 small onions, minced
1 cup crackers, roll into crumbs
Salt to taste

Boil squash for 20 minutes. Let cool. Slice the tops off, about 2-inches long. Take spoon and scoop pulp out. Mash pulp. Mix pulp and all ingredients with cracker meal until it is stiff enough to place in opening; fill the squash. Grease bottom of pan well. Place squash so the stems will not break and bake slowly to a light brown. Serve hot.

"Attractive dish and very tasty. We have had hundreds of requests for this recipe."

Green Bean Casserole

2 cans (16-ounces each) cut green beans, drained
(or 2 packages (9-ounces each) frozen cut green beans)
¾ cup milk
1 can (10 ¾-ounce) condensed cream of mushroom soup
⅛ teaspoon pepper
1 can (2.8-ounce) French fried onions

Preheat oven to 350°F. In medium bowl, combine beans, milk, soup, pepper and ½ can French fried onions; pour into 1 ½-quart casserole. Bake, uncovered for 30 minutes or until heated through. Top with remaining onions; bake, uncovered, 5 minutes or until onions are golden brown. Serves 6.

Microwave directions: Prepare green bean mixture as above; pour into 1 ½-quart microwave-safe casserole. Cook, covered, on High 8-10 minutes or until heated through. Stir beans halfway through cooking time. Top with remaining onions; cook, uncovered 1 minute. Let stand 5 minutes.

Grilled Vegetable Kabobs with Rice

½ cup commercial oil-free Italian dressing
1 tablespoon minced fresh parsley (or 1 teaspoon dried parsley flakes)
1 teaspoon dried whole basil
2 medium-size yellow squash, cut into 1-inch slices
8 small boiling onions
8 cherry tomatoes
8 medium-size fresh mushrooms
Vegetable cooking spray
2 cups hot cooked long-grain rice (cooked without salt or fat)

Combine dressing, parsley, and basil in a small bowl; cover and chill. Alternate squash, onions, tomatoes, and mushrooms on 8 skewers. Coat grill rack with cooking spray; place on grill over medium coals. Place kabobs on rack, and cook 15 minutes or until vegetables are tender, turning and basting frequently with dressing mixture. To serve, place ½ cup rice on each plate, and top with 2 vegetable kabobs. Serves 4.

Black-Eyed Peas

6 cans (15-ounces each) black eyed peas, undrained
2 cans (15-ounces each) diced tomatoes, undrained
1 small green pepper, diced
1 medium onion, diced
1 pound hot sausage
1 teaspoon oregano
Sprinkle of garlic powder
Pepper to taste

Cook sausage in 6-quart pot. Drain. Add pepper, onions, oregano and a sprinkle of garlic powder. Cook for 5 minutes. Add tomatoes and black-eyed peas. Stir well. Cover and simmer for 45 minutes.

Shirley M. Meredith, Sacred Heart Church,
Conemaugh, PA

Hash Brown Casserole

Casserole
2 pounds frozen hash brown potatoes, thawed
2 cans cream of chicken soup
(or substitute 1 can cream of chicken soup and 1 can cream of mushroom soup)
1 container (8-ounce) sour cream
½ cup chopped onion
2 cups mild cheddar cheese, grated
1 teaspoon salt
½ teaspoon pepper

Topping
2 cups crushed corn flakes
½ cup melted butter

Preheat oven to 350°F. Mix all ingredients in large bowl. Pour into a long 13x9-inch baking dish. Top with crushed corn flakes and melted butter. Bake for 50 to 60 minutes.

Barbara Jarvis, Forest Heights Methodist Church, Jackson, TN

Creamed Sweet Potatoes with Marshmallows

6 large, yellow sweet potatoes
¼ cup butter
1 ¼ cups sugar
2 teaspoons orange flavoring
Dash of black pepper
1 cup whole milk
Pinch of salt
3 eggs, well-beaten
1 cup chopped pecans and raisins
Heavy dash of pulverized ginger

Topping
Marshmallows
Crystallized red cherries

Clean sweet potatoes. Boil until very tender. Remove and peel. Cream with ¼ cup butter and 1 ¼ cups sugar. After creaming add remaining ingredients. Place in casserole dish and cook until it sets.

For topping: Cover casserole with marshmallows and brown lightly. Add crystallized red cherries between marshmallows. Serve hot.

Makes a beautiful dish.

Butter-Fried Carrots

5-6 carrots, peeled, cut lengthwise into quarters
4 cups water
¼ cup flour
½ cup butter, melted
½ teaspoon seasoned salt

In covered pan, boil carrots in water until tender, drain. Dip carrots into ¼ cup melted butter. In plastic bag combine flour and seasoned salt. Add carrots; shake to coat with flour mixture. In skillet melt ¼ cup butter until sizzling. Add carrots, cook over medium heat, turning occasionally, until all sides are golden brown (8-10 minutes). You can also deep fry them or bake in oven for "low fat."

Broccoli with Rice

1 small onion, chopped
1 tablespoon butter
1 cup instant rice
2 packages chopped broccoli
1 can cream of chicken soup
½ cup milk
1 cup cheese, grated

Preheat oven to 350°F. Sauté onion in butter. Add instant rice and cook a little with the butter and onion. Add broccoli (cooked and drained), soup, milk and cheese. Bake for 1 hour.

Tortilla Rolls

1 brick cream cheese
1 small carton sour cream
1 small can chopped green chilies
½ can green enchilada sauce
12 flour tortillas

Mix the cheese, sour cream, chilies and sauce. Chill. Spread on the tortillas and roll. Wrap in foil and chill overnight. Cut into small sections and serve.

Candied Yams

6 yellow sweet potatoes
½ stick butter
Dash of nutmeg (or cinnamon)
1 cup sugar

Take six yellow sweet potatoes, medium size. Boil 30 minutes. Peel. Slice length way about 1/5 of an inch. Place one layer potatoes in heavy baking pan. Dot with butter, sprinkle nutmeg or cinnamon and sugar over this layer. Repeat until all potatoes are used. Cover with water. Cook in 250°F oven for one hour.

Baked or Grilled Potatoes

Cubed potatoes
Chopped onions
Chopped green peppers
Butter

Preheat oven to 350°F. Cut all into small chunks, put in foil or baking dish. Add butter and bake until done (30 minutes) or put on grill in foil and cook until done. The potatoes are best cooked on grill.

Italian Style Potatoes

12 medium potatoes, cut in 1-inch cubes, medium thin
Olive oil
8 medium onions, cut in quarters
4 green peppers, sliced lengthwise
6 cloves garlic, chopped, or garlic powder
Italian seasoning, if desired

In frying pan fry potatoes in enough olive oil to keep from sticking or burning. Cook until soft. Add onions, sauté. Add peppers. Stir often. Add garlic powder (or garlic) and Italian seasoning. Cook until vegetables are soft.

Carmela Zarrillo, Interlachen Seventh-day Adventist Church, Interlachen, FL

Eggplant Parmesan

Tomato sauce
6 eggs
Bread crumbs, seasoned, Italian style
Italian seasoning
1 medium eggplant, peeled and sliced
Olive oil
Romano cheese

Preheat oven to 350°F. Cover bottom of casserole dish with tomato sauce. In bowl, beat eggs. Add bread crumbs and Italian seasoning. Dip each slice of eggplant in egg mixture draining slightly before frying in hot olive oil. Fry eggplant slightly. Layer in casserole dish with sauce, eggplant and cheese. Bake for ½-1 hour. (Usually takes about 1 hour.) Eggplant is done when it is soft.

Stir-Fry Vegetables with Sausage

1 pound hot sausage
½ cup chopped bell pepper
½ cup chopped onion
½ cup chopped celery
1 can tomatoes
Salt to taste
Pepper to taste
2 teaspoons soy sauce
1 cup cooked rice
1 cup shredded sharp cheddar cheese

Brown sausage. Add pepper, onion, celery, and tomatoes in skillet. Add salt, pepper and soy sauce; cover and cook 15 minutes. Serve over hot rice. Top with cheese. For a different flavor, add the cheese while the entrée is still in the skillet.

Country Bacon Green Beans

6-8 slices country cured bacon, reserve bacon fat
2 cans French style green beans
¼ cup vinegar
½ cup brown sugar

Fry bacon until crisp; remove from skillet. Drain, reserving fat. In large saucepan, mix green beans, vinegar, and brown sugar. Add reserved bacon fat. Cook on low heat 1 hour. Fifteen minutes before serving, crumble bacon onto beans. Serve hot.

"Every time we take this to a potluck supper, we always leave with an empty bowl and folks want the recipe. It's delicious!"

*Judy & Charlie Tripp, 1st Methodist Church,
Brownsville, TN*

Tripp Tater Salad

1 cup country ham, chopped
12 cup sweet pickles, chopped
3-4 eggs, cooked & chopped
4-5 potatoes, cooked & chopped
½ -1 cup mayonnaise
½ cup onion, chopped
Salt to taste
Pepper to taste

Mix all ingredients in large bowl. Add mayonnaise to your personal texture and taste preferences. Chill and serve.

Judy & Charlie Tripp, 1st Methodist Church, Brownsville, TN

Cheesy Ranch Potato Bake

1 pound southern style hash browns
2 cans cream of chicken soup
¾ cup sour cream
1 envelope ranch dressing mix
¾ cup shredded mozzarella cheese
1 cup shredded colby-jack cheese, ½ cup reserved for topping
½ cup melted butter, reserve ½ for topping
½ teaspoon salt
½ teaspoon pepper
2 tablespoons dried onions
1 cup crushed crackers

Preheat oven to 375°F. Add all ingredients to a bowl, mix well. Spread into a greased 9x13-inch casserole dish. Add reserved cheese to top of potato bake.

Mixed reserved butter and crushed crackers in separate bowl and sprinkle over top. Bake uncovered for 30-35 minutes or until golden brown on top. Makes 10 servings.

Holly Ard, Utah State Fair, Salt Lake City, UT

Trudy's German Potato Salad

6 slices of bacon
¾ cup chopped onion
2 tablespoons flour
1–2 tablespoons of sugar
½ teaspoon celery seed
Dash of pepper
1 ½ teaspoons salt
⅓ cup vinegar
¾ cup water
6 medium boiled potatoes

Fry bacon and drain on paper towels. Sauté onion in bacon fat until golden. Add flour, sugar, celery seed, pepper and salt. Cook low till smooth and bubbly. Remove from heat. Combine vinegar and water in a small sauce pan. Heat to a boil. Stir in potatoes and bacon. Serve warm.

Marilyn Van Ryn, Sacred Heart Cathedral Church,
Knoxville, TN

Southern Sweet Potato Casserole

<u>Casserole</u>
8-10 sweet potatoes (or canned yams)
1 cup granulated sugar
½ stick butter
2 eggs beaten
1 teaspoon vanilla
½ can sweetened evaporated milk

<u>Topping</u>
¼ cup flour
1 cup brown sugar
½ stick butter
1 cup pecans

Preheat oven to 325°F. Cook and mash the potatoes. Cool. Add sugar and butter, eggs and milk. Put into dish.

<u>For topping</u>: Mix flour, brown sugar and pecans, and then add butter. Spread on top of potatoes. Add extra pecans on top if desired. Bake uncovered for 1 hour checking frequently after 45 minutes.

Robin Bullock, Daystar International Church, Mt. Olive, AL

Pasta

Spaghetti Crust Pie

2 eggs
2 tablespoons butter
⅓ cup Parmesan cheese, grated
½ pound hamburger, cooked
1 medium onion (cooked in 2 tablespoons butter)
6 ounces spaghetti
8 ounces pizza sauce
1 ½ cups mozzarella cheese, grated

Grease a 9-inch pan. In large mixing bowl, mix eggs, butter, Parmesan cheese, hamburger and onion together. Put cooked spaghetti in bottom of greased pie pan. Spread mixture over spaghetti. Top with pizza sauce, then mozzarella cheese. Bake for 20 minutes at 350°F.

Rice Casserole

2 cups cooked rice
1 cup parsley (or 2 tablespoons dried parsley)
2 cups milk
½ pound processed American cheese
¼ teaspoon garlic salt
2 eggs
½ cup vegetable oil
Minced onion

Preheat oven to 350°F. Mix all ingredients well and pour into greased casserole dish. Bake for 45 minutes.

Angie Jones, Sulphur Well Church of Christ,
Springville, TN

Oilolio

1 pound spaghetti, thin
2 garlic bulbs, separated and skins removed
Olive oil
Grated cheese, optional

Cook spaghetti as per package instructions. Drain. In frying pan, fry garlic in olive oil until soft. Put spaghetti in bowl. Add garlic and oil. Mix well and serve. May be served with grated cheese.

Carmela Zarrillo, Interlachen Seventh-day Adventist Church, Interlachen, FL

Fried Rice

3 cups water

1 ½ teaspoons salt

1 ½ cups uncooked long grain rice

4 slices bacon, cooked & chopped

3 eggs

⅛ teaspoon pepper

2 teaspoons grated fresh ginger

3 tablespoons vegetable oil

8-ounces cooked pork, cut into thin strips

8-ounces cooked, cleaned shrimp coarsely chopped

8 green onions, finely chopped

1-2 tablespoons soy sauce

Combine water and salt in a 3-quart saucepan. Cover and let cook over high heat until boiling. Stir in rice. Cover, reduce heat and simmer until rice is tender, 15-20 minutes. Cook bacon over medium heat, stirring frequently, until crisp. Drain bacon. Remove all but 1 tablespoon of the drippings from the wok. Beat eggs and pepper with a fork. Pour ⅓ of the egg mixture into the wok. Tilt wok slightly so egg mixture covers the bottom. Cook over medium heat until eggs are set, 1-2 minutes. Remove eggs from wok, roll up and cut into thin strips. Repeat this process two more times until all eggs are cooked and cut. You may need to oil the pan between mixtures. Add the remaining 2 tablespoons of oil and the ginger to the wok. Stir-fry over medium-high heat 1 minute. Stir in the rice. Cook and stir 5 minutes. Stir in the bacon, pork, shrimp, onions and soy sauce. Cook and stir until hot throughout. Serves 6-8.

Garlic-Buttered Noodles

8 ounces medium noodles
⅓ cup butter
3 cloves garlic, slivered
1 teaspoon seasoned salt
Parsley

Cook noodles according to the directions on the package. Drain and rinse. In a small skillet heat butter and garlic over low heat until butter is melted; stir occasionally. Remove garlic. Blend mixture with salt. Pour over noodles and toss lightly to coat evenly. Garnish with chopped parsley.

Macaroni & Cheese

1 ½ cups elbow macaroni
2 tablespoons butter
2 tablespoons flour
2 cups milk
½ teaspoon salt
¼ teaspoon freshly ground black pepper
⅛ teaspoon freshly grated nutmeg
2 cups grated cheese, preferably cheddar and American (4-ounces each)

Preheat the oven to 350°F. Cook the macaroni and drain. While the macaroni is cooking, melt the butter in a saucepan. Add the flour and cook; stirring constantly (preferably with a whisk) over low heat for 2-3 minutes. Add the milk gradually mixing the ingredients to incorporate the flour mixture and make a smooth sauce. Add the salt, pepper and nutmeg. Stirring with the whisk or a wooden spoon, add the cheese and continue to cook 4-5 minutes or until the cheese has melted and the sauce is smooth. Pour the sauce over the cooked macaroni and mix them thoroughly. Place the mixture into a buttered baking dish. Bake, covered, about 30 minutes.

Macaroni Ring

3 cups macaroni, cooked tender, drain all water
3 whole eggs, beaten together
1 heaping cup grated yellow cheese
1 tablespoon chopped pimento
1 tablespoon chopped green pepper
½ teaspoon onion salt
½ teaspoon celery salt
1 teaspoon minced onion
¼ teaspoon garlic salt
½ cup canned tomatoes
½ stick melted butter
¼ teaspoon salt
½ cup milk
½ teaspoon yellow food coloring
Creamed peas, cooked
Parsley

Mix first 13 ingredients. Add yellow food coloring. Grease baking ring well and overfill with macaroni mixture. Place in pan of water and cook in medium oven. When well done, place in round dish. Fill with creamed peas. Garnish with parsley.

Pasta Primavera

2-3 cloves garlic, minced
2 small carrots, julienned
1 small eggplant, peeled and julienned
½ pound mushrooms, julienned
3 tablespoons butter
2 small zucchini, shredded
2 ounces prosciutto, julienned
1 large tomato, peeled, seeded and cut into tiny wedges
½ cup heavy cream
½ cup chopped fresh basil
Salt to taste
Freshly ground pepper to taste
12 ounces spaghetti or fettuccine
½ cup freshly grated Parmesan cheese

Sauté garlic, carrots, eggplant, and mushrooms in the butter over high flame for 2 minutes. Stir in zucchini and prosciutto. Sauté one minute longer. Add tomato wedges and cream. Simmer for 5 minutes. Stir in the basil. Season to taste with salt and pepper. Bring a large pot of salted water to a boil over a high flame. Add pasta and cook until tender but firm. Drain and transfer to a serving bowl. Toss with the sauce. Sprinkle Parmesan cheese on top. Serve immediately. Serves 4-6.

Golden Pasta Exotica

½ cup butter
4 large garlic cloves, chopped
Zest of 1 large orange
¼ cup vermouth
1 large orange, juiced
1 cup apricots, thinly sliced
¼ cup chopped basil
¼ cup chopped parsley
Salt to taste
Pepper to taste
Linguini noodles, cooked
¼ cup Parmesan cheese, grated

Cook butter and garlic cloves for 2 minutes in a covered sauce pan, medium heat. Add orange zest, vermouth and orange juice. Simmer covered an additional 5 minutes. Add apricots and basil. Simmer 3 more minutes. Remove from heat. Add chopped parsley and salt and pepper. Toss with cooked and drained linguini noodles. Sprinkle with grated Parmesan.

Rustic Lasagna

9 lasagna noodles
2 cans (8-ounce) tomato sauce
1 clove garlic, minced
1 teaspoon fresh oregano or ¼ teaspoon dried oregano
1 package (10-ounce) frozen chopped broccoli, thawed and squeezed of excess liquid
1 cup shredded carrots
1 container (15-16-ounce) part-skim ricotta cheese
¼ cup grated Parmesan cheese
1 cup shredded part-skim mozzarella cheese

Cook lasagna noodles according to package directions, but do not add salt. While noodles are cooking, preheat oven to 350°F. Spray a 13x9-inch baking dish with vegetable cooking spray; set aside. In a small bowl, combine tomato sauce, garlic and oregano. Mix well. In a medium bowl, combine broccoli, carrots, ricotta, and Parmesan. Mix well. Drain noodles in a colander. Spread ½ cup of tomato sauce in bottom of prepared dish. Place 3 noodles on top of tomato sauce. Spread half of broccoli mixture over noodles. Spoon ½ cup of tomato sauce over broccoli; place 3 noodles on top. Spread with remaining broccoli mixture; top with ½ cup of tomato sauce. Top with remaining noodles and tomato sauce; sprinkle mozzarella over top. Bake until bubbling, about 45 minutes. Place on a wire rack and cool for about 15 minutes; cut into squares.

Spaghetti Sauce

1 pound ground beef
1 onion
1 ½ teaspoons Italian seasoning
1 can tomato sauce
1 cup spaghetti sauce
Medium size tomato juice
1 ½ teaspoons garlic powder (or salt)
1 small can tomato paste

Brown ground beef and onions. Add remaining ingredients. Simmer for 2-3 hours.

Macaroni and Cheese Pie

1 cup uncooked elbow macaroni
1 can evaporated milk
1 stick (½ cup) butter, melted
1 pound cheddar cheese, grated *(I like the sharp cheddar)*
3 eggs, slightly beaten

Preheat oven to 350°F. Cook macaroni according to package directions. Drain and mix with remaining ingredients, less ¼ cup of cheese. Pour into a 1 ½-quart casserole dish and sprinkle top with remaining cheese. Bake for 30-45 minutes.

*Julia Urbanek, Sugar Land Baptist Church,
Sugar Land, TX*

Slap Yo' Momma Spaghetti

<u>Sauce</u>
2 pounds ground beef
1 large onion
½ tablespoon chopped garlic
½ teaspoon garlic salt
½ teaspoon salt
½ teaspoon cayenne pepper
½ teaspoon ground black pepper
1 can diced chilies and peppers
⅓ cup chopped bell pepper
2 cans diced tomatoes
1 can diced mushrooms
1 quart spaghetti sauce, prepared
1 tablespoon Worcestershire sauce
1 dash hot sauce

<u>Noodles</u>
3-4 quarts water
½ cup cooking oil
2 tablespoons salt
1 medium box spaghetti noodles

<u>For sauce</u>: Sauté chopped onion and add browned ground beef. Place in large pot. Add all other ingredients systematically, stirring all the while. Add a little water to the jar the sauces were in, swish around and pour into pot. Add water or extra sauce to obtain desired consistency. Cook for 45 minutes on medium, then turn down to low until ready to serve.

<u>For noodles</u>: Boil water in large pot with cooking oil and salt. When water has come to boil, add spaghetti noodles. Bring back to boil and turn down to medium heat. Cook until tender. When ready to serve, drain in colander. Place spaghetti noodles on a plate, top with sauce.

Mike Blizzard, Cornerstone Baptist Church,
Macon, GA

Desserts

Mae's Apple Pie

4-5 cups apples, peeled and sliced
½ cup (1 stick) butter
1 cup sugar
1 teaspoon cornstarch
Apple pie spice (optional)
1 teaspoon cinnamon
2 prepared pie crusts

Preheat oven to 425°F. Place apples in frying pan. Add butter.
Mix sugar, cornstarch, apple pie spice, and cinnamon together.
Add to apples and butter. Heat until hot. Pour into pie crusts.
Add top crust or strips. Bake for 25 minutes.

Mae Taylor, Tennessee Valley Fair,
Knoxville, TN

Old South Bread Pudding

½ cup sugar
½ teaspoon cinnamon
½ teaspoon salt
2 eggs
2 cups milk
2 cups cream
2 teaspoons vanilla
8 slices bread, cut in cubes (thick sliced or homemade)
½ cup seedless raisins
3 tablespoons butter, melted

Preheat oven to 350°F. Mix sugar, cinnamon and salt. Beat in eggs and slowly stir in milk, cream and vanilla. Add the bread cubes, raisins and butter. Pour into 9-inch square pan. Bake for about an hour until knife stuck near center comes out clean.

Mary McLeary, Harris Grove Methodist Church,
Humboldt, TN

Sweet Potato Cobbler

3-4 medium sweet potatoes
½-1 cup sugar, plus extra for topping
1 teaspoon vanilla
½ teaspoon cinnamon
¼ teaspoon nutmeg
1 stick butter
⅛ cup cornstarch
¼ cup water
Basic biscuit dough

Preheat oven to 350°F. Peel and cube potatoes. Cover with water and boil till fork tender, do not drain. Add sugar, vanilla, cinnamon, nutmeg and butter. Mix cornstarch with ¼ cup water, add to potato mixture. Cook on low while you make basic dough. Roll dough out. In 3-quart casserole dish add layer potatoes, part of dough, layer potatoes and so on. Finish up with dough on top. Sprinkle with sugar and dot with extra butter. Cook for 30 minutes or until dough is done.

Gary Morris, Richland Hills Baptist Church, Fort Worth, TX

Chocolate Bread Pudding

6 cups crustless French bread, cut into 1-inch cubes (almost a
1-pound loaf)
¼ cup (½ stick) unsalted butter, melted
1 large chocolate bar, chopped into pieces
1 ¾ cups whole milk
1 cup whipping cream
6 ounces unsweetened chocolate, chopped
1 cup sugar
4 large egg yolks
Whipped cream or vanilla ice cream (optional)

Preheat oven to 350°F. Butter 8x8x2-inch glass baking dish. Place
bread cubes in large bowl; drizzle with butter and toss to coat.
Transfer bread to prepared dish. Sprinkle pieces of chocolate bar
over the bread. In heavy large saucepan, bring milk and cream
to a simmer. Remove from heat. Add chopped chocolate; whisk
until melted and smooth. Whisk sugar and yolks in medium
bowl to blend. Whisk chocolate mixture into sugar mixture.
Pour custard over bread. Cover with plastic and let stand 1 hour
(some custard will not be absorbed). (Can be prepared up to 2
hours ahead. Refrigerate.) Bake pudding until just set but center

moves slightly when dish is shaken, about 35 minutes. Serve warm or at room temperature with whipped cream, if desired.

Josephine Murphy, 1st Methodist Church,
Jackson, TN

Chocolate Bread Pudding Filled With Peanut Butter Cups

<u>Bread Pudding</u>
1 teaspoon butter
4 large eggs
1 cup firmly packed light brown sugar
½ teaspoon ground cinnamon
⅛ teaspoon freshly grated nutmeg
1 teaspoon pure vanilla extract
1 cup semisweet chocolate chips, melted plus more for topping
2 cups half & half
10 sliced day-old white bread (lightly toasted and cut into ½-inch cubes)
2 cups peanut butter cups, chopped plus more for grating
½ cup milk chocolate chips

<u>Sassy Cream</u>
1 quart heavy cream
⅓ cup granulated sugar
½ teaspoon ground cinnamon
¼ teaspoon freshly grated nutmeg

<u>For bread pudding</u>: Preheat oven to 350°F. Grease a 6 cup loaf pan with the butter. Whisk the eggs, sugar, cinnamon, nutmeg, vanilla, & melted chocolate together in a large mixing bowl until smooth. Add the half and half, and mix well. Add the bread and let the mixture sit for 30 minutes, stirring occasionally. Pour half of the mixture into the prepared pan. Sprinkle the top with the unmelted chocolate chips and add chopped peanut butter cups. Pour the remaining bread mixture over the chocolate chips. Bake until the pudding is set in the center, about 55 minutes. Let cool for 5 minutes. To serve, cut the pudding into 1-inch thick slices. Top with sassy cream and garnish with additional grated peanut butter cups.

<u>For sassy cream</u>: Beat the cream in a large bowl with an electric mixer on high speed for 2 minutes. Add the sugar, cinnamon, and nutmeg and beat again until the mixture thickens and forms stiff peaks, another 1-2 minutes.

Creamsicle Jell-O ®

1 box (3-ounce) apricot Jell-O®
1 cup boiling water
½ cup orange juice
1 ½ cups non-dairy whipped topping, thawed
1 carton (8-ounce) plain yogurt

Dissolve Jell-O® in water. Add juice. Chill until it starts to gel. In bowl of electric mixer add yogurt and whipped topping to chilled mixture. Refrigerate.

"The taste reminds us of orange creamsicles."

Chocolate Sop Gravy

1 stick butter
1 cup sugar
2 heaping tablespoons flour
2 cups milk
2 heaping tablespoons chocolate
½ teaspoon vanilla

Melt butter in skillet. Add additional ingredients and cook until a gravy consistency is reached. Add the vanilla. Serve over hot homemade biscuits.

Lemon Hearts with Butter Crust and Sour Cream Topping

<u>Lemon Hearts and Butter Crust</u>
3 cups all-purpose flour
¾ cup sifted confectioners' sugar, plus 3-6 additional tablespoons
¾ cup butter, softened
¾ cup margarine, softened
1 ½ teaspoons vanilla extract
3 cups sugar
3 tablespoons cornstarch
8 large eggs, beaten
¾ cup fresh lemon juice
3 tablespoons butter, melted
Lemon peel knots, optional

<u>Sour Cream Topping</u>
1 ½ cups sour cream
2 tablespoons sugar
½ teaspoon vanilla
⅛ teaspoon salt

For lemon hearts and butter crust: Preheat oven to 350°F. Combine first 5 ingredients; beat at low speed of an electric mixer until blended. Pat mixture into a greased 13x9x2-inch baking dish. Set aside.

Combine sugar and cornstarch. Add eggs and next 2 ingredients; beat well. Pour mixture over crust.

Bake for 35-40 minutes or until set. Cool and chill well. Sift confectioners' sugar over top, cut into hearts or squares. Yield: 12 hearts or 2 ½ dozen squares.

For sour cream topping: Mix all ingredients together. Spoon a dollop on top of each heart or square when served. Garnish with lemon peel knots optional.

Colleen Peck, Utah State Fair,
Salt Lake City, UT

Caramel Apple Cheesecake

1 can (21-ounce) apple pie filling, reserve ¾ cups
1 ready-made graham cracker crust (9-ounce)
2 packages (8-ounces each) cream cheese softened
½ cup sugar
¼ teaspoon vanilla
2 eggs
¼ cup caramel topping
2 apples, thinly sliced (coated in lemon juice)
12 half pecans plus 2 tablespoons chopped pecans

Preheat oven to 350°F. Reserve ¾ cup apple pie filling. Spoon remaining filling into crust. Beat cream cheese, sugar and vanilla until smooth. Add eggs and beat well. Pour over apple filling and bake 35 minutes or until center is set. Cool. Mix reserved apple filling and caramel topping in a small saucepan. Heat about 1 minute. Arrange apple slices around outside edge of cheesecake. Spoon caramel sauce onto the cheesecake and spread evenly. Decorate with pecan halves around edge. Sprinkle with chopped pecans. Refrigerate.

Shirley M. Meredith, Sacred Heart Church, Conemaugh, PA

German Chocolate Pound Cake

1 box (18 ¼-ounce) German chocolate cake mix
1 can (15-ounce) coconut-pecan frosting
4 eggs
½ cup oil
1 cup water

Preheat oven to 350°F. Flour 12-cup tube pan or bundt pan. Mix all ingredients (including the icing) in mixer at medium speed for 2 minutes. Pour into prepared pan and bake for 55-60 minutes. Remove from oven to wire rack and allow cooling for 10 minutes. Invert onto serving plate and dust with confectioners' sugar.

Note: This makes a large cake, be sure to use the large 12-cup pan.

Alice Edwards, First Assembly of God Church,
Mexico, MO

White Chocolate Blackberry Cheesecake

<u>Crust</u>
1 cup slivered unsalted almonds
2 cups graham cracker crumbs (7 ounces)
6 tablespoons unsalted butter, melted

<u>Filling</u>
8 ounces white chocolate
4 packages (8-ounces each) cream cheese, softened
½ cup plus 2 tablespoons sugar
4 whole large eggs
2 large egg yolks
2 tablespoons all purpose flour
1 teaspoon vanilla extract
Enough blackberries to fill the bottom of the pan – about 2 cups fresh blackberries
1 bag (12-ounce) frozen blackberries
Preheat the oven to 350°F.

<u>For the crust</u>: Finely grind the almonds in a food processor. Finely grind the graham crackers in a food processor until you have 7 ounces. Melt the butter and add it to the ground mix,

blending until combined. Press this mixture over the bottom and ⅔ up the side of a 10-inch spring form pan.

For filling: Melt the chocolate in a double boiler, stirring until smooth. Remove from the heat. Beat the cream cheese with an electric mixer at medium speed until fluffy. Add sugar. Add whole eggs and yolks, one at a time, beating well at a low speed. Scrape down the bowl after each addition. Add flour and vanilla extract until just combined. Add the melted chocolate in a slow stream, beating until the filling is well combined (you may need to re-warm the chocolate slightly to loosen it up if it set up while you were doing the other tasks).

Arrange the berries in one layer over the crust. Pour the filling over the berries. Bake in the middle of the oven until the cheesecake is set 3- inches from the edge of the pan but the center of the cheesecake is still wobbly when the pan is gently shaken (about 45-55 minutes).

Run a thin knife around the edge of the cake to loosen the crust from the pan. Cool the cheesecake completely in the pan on a rack. (The cheesecake will continue to set as it cools). Serve at room temperature or chilled.

Optional: You may choose to garnish the cheesecake slices with a few berries.

Sandra Scott, Dixie Classic Fair,
Winston-Salem, NC

Cream Cheese Pie

<u>Pie</u>
1 cup confectioners' sugar
1 container (8-ounce) cream cheese, softened
4 ounces non-dairy whipped topping
1 graham cracker crust

<u>Topping</u>
1 package strawberry glaze
1 quart fresh strawberries, sliced

Mix sugar and cream cheese, then add whipped topping. Pour into crust.

<u>Substitutions</u>: Peach glaze and fresh peaches or your favorite pie filling. Apple pie filling is great with caramel ice cream topping drizzled on top of pie.

Lisa Goodale, Soul's Harbor PH Church,
Hartsville, SC

Cocoa Drop Cookies

½ cup sugar
¾ cup (scant) melted shortening or ⅝ cup oil
½ cup cocoa
1 egg
¾ cup sour milk or (¾ cup milk + 1 tablespoon of vinegar)
2 teaspoons vanilla
¼ teaspoon cream of tartar
Pinch of salt
½ teaspoon baking soda
2 ¼ cups flour

Combine sugar, shortening, cocoa and egg. Add alternately the remaining dry and wet ingredients; sour milk, vanilla, cream of tartar, salt, baking soda and flour.

"This recipe was passed down from my grandma, Lola Metzger."

Beth Topping, Pleasant Hill Church,
Bronson, MI

Praline Wafer Dessert

45 vanilla wafers
2 cups flaked coconut
⅔ cup pecans, chopped
⅔ cup brown sugar
6 tablespoons butter
1 package instant vanilla pudding
1 ½ cups milk
1 cup heavy cream, whipped

Arrange 21 whole vanilla wafers in bottom of 9-inch springform pan. Cut a slight portion off each remaining vanilla wafer to form straight edge. Place those wafers, straight edge down, around edge of pan, overlapping them in a clockwise fashion.

Combine coconut, pecans, brown sugar, and butter in a skillet. Cook over low heat, stirring constantly, until butter is melted. Continue to cook and stir until mixture browns lightly, about 5 minutes.

Pour onto baking sheet to cool. Break coconut mixture into coarse crumbles. Reserve 1 cup. Sprinkle remaining crumbs over wafer base. Prepare pudding with milk as directed on label.

Fold in whipped cream. Turn mixture into pan, spreading gently to the edges of the standing wafers. Sprinkle with reserved crumbs. Chill for 4 hours or overnight. Cut in wedges to serve. Serves 6-8

Gay Gregson, West Jackson Baptist Church,
Jackson, TN

Gob Cake

<u>Cake</u>
1 box Devil's food cake mix
¼ cup oil
3 eggs
1 small box chocolate pudding mix (instant)

<u>Gob Icing</u>
2 boxes sugar free vanilla pudding
1 cup sugar substitute
2 ½ cups skim milk
1 cup butter-flavored solid shortening
2 teaspoons vanilla
Confectioners' sugar

<u>For cake</u>: Preheat oven to 350°F. Beat all ingredients till smooth. Spread on 2 small cookie sheets (10x15x¾-inch) lined with wax paper. Bake until done (toothpick inserted in middle comes out clean).

<u>For icing</u>: Beat until thick. Refrigerate. Take 1 cookie sheet turn out on platter, remove wax paper. Spread icing on cake. Top with other layer. Remove wax paper. Sprinkle with confectioners' sugar, if you would like.

Shirley M. Meredith, Sacred Heart Church,
Conemaugh, PA

Red, White & Blue Cake

1 box lemon cake mix, batter prepared as directed on box
Red and blue food coloring
1 box white cake mix, batter prepared as directed on box
About ½ jar of commercial lemon curd
1 large container non-dairy whipped topping, slightly softened

Prepare lemon cake mix according to package directions. Divide batter into two bowls. In one bowl, add about ½ bottle of red food coloring; adjust as necessary to obtain desired color. In second bowl, add about ½ bottle of blue food coloring; adjust as necessary to obtain desired color. Pour each batter into individually prepared, 8-inch round cake pans. Bake as directed until done.

In the meantime, prepare white cake mix according to package directions. Pour batter into two prepared, 8-inch round cake pans. Bake as directed. (You will use only one of these layers; set the other aside for strawberry shortcake!)

After all layers are baked and cooled, assemble cake. Place red layer on serving plate. Spread with a light coating of lemon curd. Place one white layer on top of the red layer. Spread with a light coating of lemon curd. Place blue layer on top of the white layer. Frost cake top and sided generously with non-dairy whipped topping. Refrigerate. Serve chilled!

"A beautiful and delicious cake to serve on July 4th or at a family picnic!"

Kathy Harris, First Baptist Church,
Nashville, TN

Pineapple Surprise

1 box yellow cake mix
1 small box sugar-free instant vanilla pudding mix
1 package (8-ounce) low fat cream cheese, softened
2 cups skim milk
1 large can pineapple tidbits in own juice, drained
1 container (8-ounce) non-dairy whipped topping

Preheat oven to 350°F. Mix cake as directed. Bake in 9x13-inch pan lightly greased and floured. Bake for 20 minutes – or until done. Cool. Be sure cream cheese is room temperature. Beat with small bit of milk. Gradually add the remaining 2 cups of milk. Add pudding. Mix until thick. Then pour on cooled cake. Add the drained pineapple on top of pudding. Top with whipped topping. Top with nuts. Refrigerate overnight.

Larry & Brenda Wisse, Trinity Lutheran Church,
Marysville, OH

Strawberry-Banana Shortcake

2 quarts strawberries, washed and stemmed
3 bananas (firm but ripe)
1 angel food cake (or regular shortcake)
Non-dairy whipped topping

Thickly slice the strawberries. Leave very wet to increase juice. Sweeten to taste and refrigerate a few hours before serving. When ready to serve, thickly slice bananas and add to strawberry mixture. Stir so as to slightly mash some of the fruit. Place a big chunk of angel food cake in each dessert bowl. Cover cake with fruit and juice mixture. Top with a big dollop of whipped cream. Serve immediately.

"You can certainly use blackberries, blueberries, peaches, even pineapple to replace bananas...or what the heck....add all the different fruit you desire. Makes some good eatin'!"

*Linda Dotson-Wooley, Mt. Zion Baptist Church,
Hendersonville, TN*

Divinity

3 cups sugar
¾ cup light corn syrup
½ cup water
2 egg whites
1 teaspoon almond extract

Place sugar, corn syrup and water in heavy saucepan. Over medium heat, cook to hard ball stage (248°F). Remove from heat and let stand until temperature drops to 220°F WITHOUT STIRRING.

Place egg whites in bowl and whip until soft peaks form (about 1 minute). Gradually add syrup in a fine stream (about 2 ½ minutes). Reduce speed. Add almond extract. Continue whipping 20-25 minutes or until it starts to become dry.

Drop mixture from spoon (move fast as it hardens quickly) onto wax paper to form balls.

Paul McDade, Ohio State Fair, Columbus, OH

Dump Cake

1 can crushed pineapple
1 can cherry pie filling
1 yellow cake mix
1 stick butter

Preheat oven to 350°F. Dump pineapple in cake pan. Dump cherry pie filling on top of pineapple. Dump dry cake mix on top of fruit. Cover cake mix with butter. Bake until golden brown.

Mary Ann Kuhner,
Ashland Area Presbyterian Ministries,
Flatwoods, KY

Angel Food Cake

Cake
12 egg whites
1 ½ teaspoons cream of tartar
1 ½ cups sugar, divided
1 ½ teaspoons vanilla
½ teaspoon almond extract
1 cup sifted cake flour
¼ teaspoon salt

Pineapple Filling
1 package (4-ounce) fat free, sugar free instant vanilla pudding
1 can (20-ounce) crushed pineapple in juice, undrained
1 cup non-dairy whipped topping
10 fresh strawberries, optional

For cake: Preheat oven to 375°F. In large mixing bowl, beat egg whites with cream of tartar at high speed until foamy. Add ¾ cup of sugar, 2 tablespoons at a time, beating constantly until sugar is dissolved and egg whites are glossy and stand in soft peaks. Beat in flavorings.

Sift together flour, remaining sugar and salt. Sift about ½ cup of the flour mixture over whites and gently fold just until flour disappears. Repeat folding in remaining flour mixture, ½ cup at a time. Pour into ungreased 10x4-inch tube pan. Gently cut through batter with metal spatula.

Bake in oven until top springs back when lightly touched with finger, about 30-40 minutes. Invert cake in pan on funnel or bottle neck. Cool completely, about 1 ½ hours. With narrow spatula or knife, loosen cake from pan and gently shake onto serving plate. Prepare pineapple filling and fill cake.

For filling: Mix dry pudding and pineapple with juice in medium bowl. Gently stir in whipped topping.

Cut cake horizontally into 3 layers. Place bottom cake layer, cut side up, on a serving plate; top with 1 ⅓ cups of the pineapple mixture. Cover with middle cake layer and additional 1 cup of remaining pudding mixture. Top with remaining cake layer. Spread with remaining mixture.

Refrigerate at least 1 hour. Top with whole strawberries just before serving. (This is just to make the cake look prettier). Store leftover dessert in refrigerator.

Audra Fensermaker, Clarion County Fair,
New Bethlehem, PA

Coal Black Cake

2 cups flour
2 cups sugar
2 teaspoons baking soda
1 teaspoon salt
1 cup cocoa
1 cup oil
2 eggs
2 cups boiling water
1 teaspoon vanilla

Preheat oven to 350°F. Mix dry ingredients. Add liquid ingredients. Mix until smooth. Pour in greased 12x15-inch pan. Bake for 25 minutes.

Shana Cumm, Saratoga County Fair,
Ballston Spa, NY

Grand Champion Sponge Cake

1 ¼ cups sifted flour
1 cup sugar
½ teaspoon salt
½ teaspoon baking powder
6 egg whites
1 teaspoon cream of tartar
½ cup sugar
6 egg yolks
¼ cup water
1 teaspoon vanilla
½ teaspoon almond

Preheat oven to 350°F. Sift together flour, 1 cup sugar, salt and baking powder. In large mixing bowl, beat egg whites until fluffy; add cream of tartar. Gradually beat in ½ cup sugar, a little at a time, until whites form stiff peaks. In small bowl, combine egg yolks, water, vanilla, almond and dry ingredients. Beat at medium-high speed for 4 minutes until mixture is light and fluffy. Fold yolk mixture gently, but thoroughly into beaten egg whites. Bake in 10-inch tube pan for 45 minutes.

Plainfield Farmers Fair, Pen Argyl, PA

Coconut Cream Pie

½ package (15-ounce) refrigerated pie crusts
½ cup sugar
¼ cup cornstarch
2 cups half & half
4 egg yolks
3 tablespoons butter
1 cup sweetened flaked coconut
1 ½ teaspoons vanilla extract plus 1 teaspoon
2 cups whipping cream
⅓ cup sugar
Toasted coconut, garnish

Shape 1 pie crust into a 9-inch pie plate according to package directions. Fold edges under, and crimp. Prick bottom and sides of pie crust with a fork. Bake according to package directions for a one-crust pie. Combine ½ cup sugar and cornstarch in a heavy saucepan. Whisk half & half and egg yolks. Gradually whisk egg mixture into sugar mixture. Bring to a boil over medium heat, whisking constantly. Boil 1 minute. Remove from heat. Stir in butter, 1 cup coconut, and 1 teaspoon vanilla. Cover with plastic wrap, placing plastic wrap directly on filling in pan. Let stand 30 minutes. Spoon custard mixture into prepared crust. Cover and chill 30 minutes or until set. Beat whipping cream at high speed with an electric mixer until frothy. Gradually add ⅓ cup sugar and remaining 1 ½ teaspoons vanilla, beating until soft peaks form. Spread or pipe whipped cream over pie filling. Garnish, if desired. Yield: Makes 6 to 8 servings

Gail Chandler, Sulphur Well Church of Christ,
Springville, TN

Tennessee Pudding

Date loaf
1 tablespoon soda
½ cup buttermilk
2 sticks butter
2 cups sugar
4 large eggs, beaten
3 ½ cups flour
1 cup chopped toasted pecans
1 cup chopped dates
1 cup coconut
1 teaspoon vanilla

Sauce
1 ½ cups orange juice
½ cup sugar
¼ cup brown sugar or ¼ cup sorghum
¼ cup butter

For date loaf: Preheat oven to 300°F. Dissolve soda in buttermilk. Cream butter and sugar and add to buttermilk. Add eggs and flour. Blend well. Add nuts, dates, coconut and vanilla. Bake in a greased tube pan for 1 ½ hours. Pour sauce over while hot. Cool in pan before serving.

<u>For sauce</u>: Heat all ingredients in heavy bottomed saucepan until dissolved. Boil for one minute. Pour over the pudding. When serving, top with whipped topping.

Calvin Murphy, Jr., Forest Heights Methodist Church, Jackson, TN

Best Pecan Pie Ever

1 stick butter
1 cup sugar
1 cup light corn syrup
3 eggs (beaten)
1 cup chopped pecan
1 unbaked pie shell (9-inch)

Preheat oven to 350°F. Melt butter but do not brown. Mix in sugar and corn syrup until sugar dissolves. Stir in eggs. Mix well. Stir in pecans. Pour into pie shell. Bake 1 hour.

Joanne Goldstein, Jackson, TN

and sauce is bubbly. Dust with confectioners' sugar and serve immediately with whipped cream or ice cream.

Libby Murphy, 1st Methodist Church,
Jackson, TN

Orange Glow Cheesecake

Crust
2 ½ cups graham cracker crumbs
½ cup margarine, melted
½ cup sugar

Filling
5 packages (8-ounces each) cream cheese (room temperature)
1 ¾ cups sugar
3 tablespoons all-purpose flour
3 teaspoons grated lemon zest
2 teaspoons grated orange zest
1 teaspoon vanilla
5 large eggs
2 egg yolks
¼ cup heavy cream

Topping
1 cup sour cream
2 cups orange juice
½ cup sugar
⅛ teaspoon yellow food color
¼ teaspoon orange extract
2 heaping tablespoons cornstarch
½ cup cold water

Garnish
Orange zest curls
Orange wedges
Sweetened whipped cream

For crust: Preheat oven to 375°F. In medium sized bowl, toss crumbs with margarine and sugar until moistened. Pour into 10-inch spring form pan. Press mixture evenly over bottom and up side of pan. Bake 5 minutes or until golden brown. Cool on wire rack.

For filling: Increase oven temperature to 450°F. In large bowl with electric mixer at high speed, beat cream cheese, sugar, flour, lemon and orange zests and vanilla until blended. Beat in eggs and egg yolks one at a time. Beat until smooth, occasionally scraping bowl with spatula. Blend in heavy cream. Pour into prepared pan. Cover outside bottom and sides of pan with aluminum foil and set into a large pan half full of hot water. Bake 10 minutes. Lower oven temperature to 250°F. Bake 1 hour longer. Turn off oven. Let stand two hours in the oven without opening the door. Remove to wire rack, run metal spatula around top edge to loosen from pan. Cool completely. With back of spoon, spread sour cream from topping ingredients evenly over top of cake within ½-inch of edge. Refrigerate 3 hours or overnight. Remove from pan.

For topping: Combine orange juice, sugar, food coloring and orange extract. Bring to a boil. Dissolve cornstarch in cold water. Stir into hot orange mixture. Cook and stir with whisk until mixture is thickened and smooth. Cool overnight in refrigerator. Whisk orange sauce until smooth, spoon ½ of sauce over sour cream to within ½-inch edge of sour cream. Save rest of sauce to spoon onto plate when serving. Garnish as desired. Decorate around outside edge with sweetened whipped cream.

Phyllis Eckler, The Great New York State Fair, Syracuse, NY

Chocolate Pumpkin Cookies

1 pumpkin to carve
2 cups flour plus 2 tablespoons
1 teaspoon baking powder
1 teaspoon pumpkin pie spice
½ teaspoon soda
¼ teaspoon salt
½ cup butter
1 cup brown sugar
1 egg
1 cup yam, baked and peeled (then mashed in food processor until smooth)
2 teaspoons vanilla
Bag of chocolate balls, unwrapped
Chocolate bars to melt

Preheat oven to 350°F. Carve out large eyes, etc. from pumpkin. Place scrap pieces in baking dish, cover with foil and bake for 1 hour. Allow pumpkin to cool, and then scrape flesh into food processor and blend. Measure 1 cup pumpkin puree for cookies.

Preheat oven to 375°F. Stir together flour, baking powder, pumpkin pie spice, soda and salt. In bowl of electric mixer beat butter and brown sugar till fluffy. Add egg, pumpkin, yam and vanilla, and then beat well. Add dry ingredients, mix until barely combined. Drop globs of dough onto greased baking sheet. Bake for 8-10 minutes. Place a chocolate ball on each cookie. Melt chocolate bar pieces in baggie in microwave until soft. Cut a corner of the bag and make a chocolate design on top of each cookie/ chocolate ball.

Marci and Keziah Roderer, Utah State Fair,
Salt Lake City, UT

Pineapple Peach Star Upside Down Cake

<u>Cake</u>
1 ½ cups flour
2 ½ teaspoons baking powder
½ teaspoon salt
⅔ cup butter
1 ½ teaspoons vanilla
1 ¾ cups sugar
2 eggs
1 ½ cups milk

<u>Filling</u>
1 can pineapple rings, drained
1 star fruit, sliced (or golden kiwi)
3 peaches, peeled and sliced
2 tablespoons butter
⅓ cup brown sugar
1 tablespoon water

<u>Garnish</u>
Caramel sauce Cherries
Non-dairy whipped cream

Combine flour, baking powder, and salt in separate bowl and set aside. Cream the butter, vanilla, and sugar in a large bowl. Then add eggs one at a time to sugar mixture. Add flour mixture and milk, mix. In Dutch oven lined with parchment paper. Arrange fruit. Melt butter, brown sugar, and water in separate pan. When mixture is syrupy, pour over fruit. Pour cake batter on top. Cook in Dutch oven over low propane on bottom and 18 coals on top for 30-35 minutes. Once cooled invert and garnish with caramel sauce, cherries and whip cream.

Dana Hancock & David Jones, Utah State Fair,
Salt Lake City, UT

RazzCherry Pie

<u>Extra-flaky Pastry</u>
2 cups flour
1 teaspoon salt
1 tablespoon sugar
¾ cup solid shortening (butter-flavored)
¼ cup ice water
1 egg
1 tablespoon vinegar

<u>"Razz" – Cherry Pie Filling</u>
1 package (10-ounce) frozen raspberries, thawed and drained (liquid reserved)
2 cups pitted, canned or frozen cherries, thawed and drained (liquid reserved)
4 tablespoons cornstarch
1 cup sugar
Dash salt
½ teaspoon almond extract
½ teaspoon orange zest
Dash cinnamon
1 tablespoon butter, chilled
1 egg white

For pastry: Preheat oven to 425°F. Sift together flour, salt, and sugar; cut shortening into flour mixture. In small bowl, beat together ice water, egg, and vinegar. One tablespoon at a time, sprinkle liquid mixture over flour mixture and fluff with fork. Cover and chill while preparing pie filling.

For filling: Add enough water to raspberry and cherry juice to make 1 ½ cups. In a medium-size saucepan, combine the 1 ½ cups liquid with cornstarch, sugar, and salt; stir to dissolve. Cook over low heat, stirring, until mixture is thick and clear. Add raspberries, cherries, almond extract, orange zest, and cinnamon and stir gently. Divide prepared pastry in half. Roll out on floured surface. Line pastry in a 9-inch pie plate; pour in pie filling. Top filling with chilled butter, divided into 6-7 pieces. Roll out other half of pastry. Place over pie. Seal and crimp. Brush surface of crust with beaten mixture of 1 egg white and 1 tablespoon cold water. Yield: One 9-inch pie.

Carol Bartholomew, Utah State Fair,
Salt Lake City, UT

Tropical Dream Pie

<u>Crust</u>
2 cups gingersnap crumbs
3 tablespoons butter, melted
2 tablespoons sugar

<u>Ganache</u>
8 ounces quality white chocolate
1 teaspoon lime zest
2 tablespoons heavy cream

<u>Filling</u>
2 cups reconstituted Saco buttermilk
½ cup fresh lime juice
4 egg yolks
1 egg
⅓ cup corn starch, sifted
1 tablespoon lime zest
½ cup cream of coconut
¼ cup shredded coconut
½ teaspoon pineapple extract
1 ⅓ cups ultra fine sugar, divided

Topping
1 ½ cups whipping cream
3 tablespoons ultra fine sugar
½ teaspoon rum extract

For crust: Preheat oven to 350°F. Mix ingredients together in a small bowl. Press mixture into 8-inch pie pan. Bake for 10 minutes. Cool completely.

For ganache: Place ingredients in a small microwaveable bowl. Heat on 50% power for 2 minutes. Stir until smooth. Pour into bottom of pie pan covering bottom evenly. Place in freezer for 30 minutes or until ganache has set. Remove from freezer and set aside.

For filling: Whip together egg, egg yolks and ⅔ cup of the sugar in a medium sized bowl. Mix buttermilk, cream of coconut and corn starch in a 2 ½-quart saucepan, bring to a simmer over medium heat, stirring constantly. Whisk milk mixture into eggs and sugar mixture. Whisk in remaining sugar. Pour mixture back into saucepan and bring to a boil over medium heat, stirring constantly. Boil for 8 minutes. Remove from heat and add coconut, pineapple extract and lime juice. Let cool to lukewarm. Pour over ganache in pie pan. Smooth out top. Refrigerate until set.

For topping: Beat all ingredients until stiff. Top pie with toasted coconut and lime zest if desired.

Jeanine Mower Anderson, Utah State Fair,
Salt Lake City, UT

Mix u Berry Pie

Crust
2 ½ cups flour
1 teaspoon salt
1 teaspoon sugar
1 cup vegetable shortening (can use butter flavored)
½ cup cold water

Filling
1 cup blackberries
1 cup strawberries
1 cup blueberries
1 cup fresh pineapple
1 cup fresh tangelo
½ cup cornstarch
1 teaspoon almond extract
½ cup sugar or sugar substitute
¼ teaspoon almond extract

Preheat oven to 350°F. Combine blackberries, strawberries, blueberries, pineapple and tangelo. In a large bowl, add cornstarch and almond extract. Stir well. Spoon into prepared piecrust. Roll out top crust. Place top crust over filling. Trim edge. Press between thumb and forefinger to make stand up edge. Cut slits in crust. Bake 40 minutes until crust is golden brown. Cool completely on wire rack.

<u>Crust</u>: Combine flour, salt, sugar, in large bowl. Cut in shortening using pastry blender or 2 knives until mixture forms pea-sized pieces. Sprinkle with water, 1 tablespoon at a time. Toss with fork until mixture stays together. Press to form a ball. Press dough between bands to form a 5-6 inch disk. Lightly flour work surface and rolling pin. Roll dough in short strokes starting in middle of disk. Rotate dough ¼ turn to right. Sprinkle more flour under dough and rolling pin as necessary to prevent sticking. Roll dough into ⅛-inch thick circle. Carefully lift dough from work surface. Place over 10-inch Dutch oven. Do not stretch dough. Trim crust. Flute as desired.

Rosa and Marisela Sanchez, Utah State Fair,
Salt Lake City, UT

Keebler® Fudge Stick Cookie Cake with Boo Berries

1 package chocolate fudge cake mix
2% milk
Butter
2 containers (16-ounces each) chocolate fudge frosting
2 packages Keebler® fudge cookie sticks
1 package (6-ounce) fresh blueberries (boo berries)
1 piece (18-inches) of Halloween ribbon, optional

Mix cake mix following package directions substituting 2% milk for water and butter for oil. Grease and flour two 8-inch round cake pans. Bake as directed. When cake is done let cool for 5 minutes. Remove from pans and cool on plates. Place in freezer for one hour. Remove cakes from freezer. Frost top of bottom cake and stack. Frost sides and top of cake. Place cookie sticks around cake sides. Alternate cookie height, one even with bottom of cake, next cookie even with top edge. Press flat side of cookie to cake sides using slight pressure each time. Continue pressing cookies around sides of cake until entire cake sides are covered. Lightly press, washed and dried blueberries on top of cake.

<u>Optional</u>: Center Halloween ribbon on outside of cookies. Overlap ends and secure with a spot of glue. (Ribbon is not edible.)

Colleen Peck, Utah State Fair,
Salt Lake City, UT

Carrot Pudding

1 cup brown sugar
¾ cup shortening
2 cups all purpose flour, sifted
2 eggs
1 ½ cups applesauce
2 teaspoons salt
2 teaspoons cinnamon
2 teaspoons nutmeg
2 ½ teaspoons baking powder
½ teaspoon baking soda
1 ½ tablespoons water
3 tablespoons lemon juice
2 cups grated carrots
2 cups raisins

Preheat oven to 350°F. In a medium bowl, mix first 12 ingredients. Add carrots and raisins. Bake in oven for 30-40 minutes in oblong cake pan. Top with whipped cream or ice cream and serve.

Carmel Icing

½ cup margarine
1 cup brown sugar
3 tablespoons milk
1 box (16-ounce) confectioners' sugar
1 teaspoon vanilla

Melt margarine in saucepan. Add brown sugar and milk. Bring to a boil. (Don't cook – just bring to a boil.) Remove from heat and cool slightly. Add confectioners' sugar. (It probably won't take the whole pound.) Add 1 teaspoon vanilla. Pour or spread. I put this icing over French vanilla cake.

"It's delicious."

Sandra Hill, Union Cumberland Presbyterian Church,
Farragut, TN

Chess Cake Bars

1 stick butter, melted
1 box yellow butter cake mix
3 eggs
1 box confectioners' sugar
1 package (8-ounce) cream cheese

Preheat oven to 350°F. Melt butter in 9x13-inch pan. Pour melted butter into cake mix; add 1 egg. Mix well. (Batter will be stiff). Pat into cake pan.

In bowl of an electric mixer beat sugar, cream cheese and 2 eggs. Pour over cake mix batter. Bake 35-45 minutes. Sides will be crumbly and middle will be soft. Freezes well.

Sandra Hill, Union Cumberland Presbyterian Church,
Farragut, TN

Graham Cracker Cookies

1 stick of margarine
1 stick of butter
½ cup sugar
1 package graham crackers, broken into pieces
¾ cup pecans, chopped

Preheat oven to 250°F. Boil ingredients in a small saucepan for 3 minutes. Spread graham crackers (broken into pieces) on a cookie sheet. Spoon the mixture over the crackers and sprinkle ¾ cup chopped pecans over the mixture. Bake 15 minutes. Let cool for 5 minutes on cookie sheet. Remove cookies to wax paper to finish cooling. Store in airtight container.

Sandra Hill, Union Cumberland Presbyterian Church, Farragut, TN

Caramel-Pecan-Pretzel Candies

1 package mini pretzels (or small squares)
1 package (13-ounce) Rolo® candies (exactly 63 candies)
1 package pecan halves

Preheat oven to 250°F. Cover a cookie sheet with aluminum foil and place pretzels individually to form one layer only. Place one Rolo® on top of each pretzel. Bake for 4 minutes or until the candies softened. Immediately remove from the oven and quickly place a pecan half on top of a candy and push down to squish the chocolate into the pretzel and flatten out. Cool for 20 minutes, then place uncovered in refrigerator for about 20 minutes to set.

Gail Chandler, Sulphur Well Church of Christ,
Springville, TN

Charleston Coconut Pie

4 eggs, beaten
½ cup self-rising flour
1 ⅓ cups sugar
½ stick butter or margarine, melted
2 cups milk
1 teaspoon vanilla
1 can (8-ounce) flake coconut

Preheat oven to 350°F. Beat all ingredients together and pour into greased 10-inch pie plate. Bake 45 minutes. (Even though the filling seems unsettled, do not cook longer.) Refrigerate until settled.

Sandra Hill, Union Cumberland Presbyterian Church, Farragut, TN

Ice Cream Sandwich Cake

2 boxes ice cream sandwiches
1 jar caramel topping
1 container non-dairy whipped topping

Put one layer of ice cream sandwiches in a 9x13-inch dish. Add ½ jar of caramel topping, then ½ container of whipped topping. Repeat layers. Top with crushed candy of choice. (Crushed Heath® Bars recommended.) Freeze until ready to serve. Let stand a few minutes for ease of service. Recommend that preparation be done the day before serving to allow the caramel to soak into the ice cream sandwiches.

Susan White, West Jackson Baptist Church,
Jackson, TN

Chocolate Pie

1 cup sugar
2 tablespoons cocoa
3 heaping tablespoons flour
1 ½ cups warm milk
3 egg yolks, beaten
1 prepared pie crust
Meringue or non-dairy whipped topping, optional

Mix first 3 ingredients together until smooth. Add about half of milk. Add eggs that have been beaten with a fork. Add rest of the milk. Cook on low heat, stirring constantly until thick. Beat with mixer to make smooth and pour into a piecrust. You can make a meringue if you like or use whipped topping when ready to serve.

Susan White, West Jackson Baptist Church,
Jackson, TN

5 Layer Bars

1 stick butter
1 ¼ cups graham cracker crumbs
1 small can sweetened condensed milk
1 cup coconut
1 cup chopped pecans
1 cup semi-sweet chocolate chips

Preheat oven to 350°F. Melt butter in a 13x9-inch cake pan. Spread graham crackers evenly over bottom. Spread sweetened condensed milk over graham crackers crumbs. Spread coconut over milk, nuts over coconuts and chocolate chips over nuts. Bake until mixture has bubbles in the middle. Approximately 20 minutes.

Susie Mitchell, Mt. Sinai Baptist Church,
Buchanan, TN

Pineapple Pie

1 can (5 ¼-ounce) crushed pineapple, undrained
1 container (8-ounce) low fat sour cream
1 large package low fat vanilla pudding
1 low fat sugar-free pie crust
1 container non-dairy whipped topping

Mix and place in pie crust. Top with whipped topping. Place in refrigerator for one hour.

Susan White, West Jackson Baptist Church,
Jackson, TN

Pecan Squares

2 cups all purpose flour
⅔ cups confectioners' sugar
¾ cups soften butter
½ cup brown sugar, firmly packed
½ cup honey
⅔ cup butter
3 tablespoons whipping cream
3 ½ cups pecans

Preheat oven to 350°F. Mixed together the above ingredients with fork or pastry blender until mixture resembles coarse meal. Pat batter on bottom and 1 ½ inches up sides of a 13x9-inch lightly greased pan. Bake for 20 minutes or until edges are lightly brown. Let cool.

Bring brown sugar, honey, butter and whipping cream to a boil. Stir in pecans, and pour hot filling into prepared crust. Bake for 25-30 minutes. Cool completely before cutting into 2-inch squares. Makes 28 squares.

Susie Mitchell, Mt. Sinai Baptist Church, Buchanan, TN

Cinnamon Candy

2 ½ cups sugar
1 cup light colored syrup
1 cup water
1 teaspoon cinnamon oil (in Tennessee we have to ask for it at a pharmacy)
1 teaspoon red food coloring

Mix sugar, syrup, and water in heavy bottomed pan. Bring to a boil, stirring occasionally. Keep boiling until mixture reaches the hard crack stage (300°F-310°F on candy thermometer). Remove from heat; add cinnamon oil and food coloring. <u>Stand back</u> and stir quickly. Pour onto a cookie sheet that has been sifted with powdered sugar. Tilt cookie sheet to even up candy. Sift more powdered sugar on top of candy. In approximately 15 minutes, candy will be ready to break up. Enjoy!

*Gail Chandler, Sulphur Well Church of Christ,
Springville, TN*

Carrot Muffins

1 ½ cups all purpose flour

1 teaspoon baking powder

1 teaspoon baking soda

1 teaspoon cinnamon

½ teaspoon salt

½ teaspoon nutmeg

¼ teaspoon ground cloves

¼ teaspoon ground allspice

2 large eggs

¾ cup sugar

1 ½ cups carrots, firmly packed and finely shredded

¼ cup orange juice

5 tablespoons warm melted unsalted butter or vegetable oil

½ cup coarsely chopped walnuts or pecans

½ cup raisins

⅓ cup shredded coconut, optional

Preheat oven to 400°F. Line a 12-cup muffin pan with paper cups. Whisk first 8 ingredients in medium mixing bowl. In a large mixing bowl whisk eggs and sugar. Add carrots. Let stand for 10 minutes. Stir orange juice, melted butter, nuts, raisins and coconut. Add the flour mixture and fold just until the dry ingredients are moistened. Do not over mix; the batter should not be smooth. Divide among muffin cups. Bake 15-18 minutes or until a toothpick comes out clean. Let cool on rack.

Anna Murphy, Forest Heights Methodist Church, Jackson, TN

Raspberry Chocolate Mousse Cups

Cream cheese filling
1 pint whipping cream
1 package (8-ounce) cream cheese, softened
1 cup confectioners' sugar
1 teaspoon vanilla
1 teaspoon raspberry extract
⅓ cup cocoa

Chocolate cups
1 package (12-ounce) semi-sweet chocolate chips
1 package (12-ounce) white chocolate chips
Balloons Raspberries Whipped cream

For cream cheese filling: Whip cream until soft peaks form; sweeten with ¼ cup confectioners' sugar. Combine next 5 ingredients. Fold cream and cream cheese mixtures together. Chill mixture until firm enough to put into pastry bag (with a large star tip).

For chocolate cups: Melt chocolate chips according to package directions. Put the melted white chocolate chips into a zip lock bag, cut a small hole in the corner of the bag. Blow up balloons.

Dip balloons in the melted semi-sweet chocolate chips let excess chocolate drip off. Drizzle the white chocolate from bag onto the chocolate dipped balloon. Use a toothpick to swirl the chocolates together. Refrigerate cups until firm. Pop balloon and remove balloon. Pipe the mousse into cups, alternating with fresh raspberries. Top with whipped cream and fresh raspberries.

Annie Broadbent, Utah State Fair,
Salt Lake City, UT

Rum Cakes

<u>Cake</u>
2 angel food cakes (13-ounces each)

<u>Sauce</u>
2 sticks margarine
1 box (16-ounce) confectioners' sugar
4 ounces rum

<u>Topping</u>
2 cups ground pecans
2 cups ground vanilla wafers

<u>For cake</u>: Slice horizontally and cut in circles with a small cookie or biscuit cutter

<u>For sauce</u>: Melt margarine in double boiler. Add confectioners' sugar and rum.

<u>For topping</u>: Dip angel food in rum sauce to coat, evenly. Roll in topping and let sit on waxed paper to firm up a little. Store in tin or airtight container. May be frozen.

*Gail Chandler, Sulphur Well Church of Christ,
Springville, TN*

Melt-A-Ways

<u>Cake</u>
1 box yellow cake mix
⅓ cup oil
3 eggs
1 ¼ cups orange juice

<u>Dunking Sauce</u>
1 box (16-ounce) confectioners' sugar
¼ cup lemon juice, freshly squeezed
½ cup orange juice

Preheat oven to 350°F. Grease and flour petite muffin pans. In a large mixing bowl, combine the first four ingredients. Fill pans ⅔ full. Bake for 10-12 minutes. While baking, prepare dunking sauce (be prepared to double this if necessary, I usually do). Mix the confectioners' sugar, lemon juice and orange juice and beat until smooth. As soon as muffins are done, dunk in sauce and set on wax paper until firm. (Best if made the night before, so they have time to set up.) One cake mix makes about 50 petite muffins.

Note: The more petite muffin pans you have, the easier to fill and bake.

*Gail Chandler, Sulphur Well Church of Christ,
Springville, TN*

Banana Split Cake

Maraschino cherries
Chocolate syrup
Nuts
2 cups graham cracker crumbs
1 stick butter, melted
2 containers (8-ounces each) cream cheese
Sugar
1 teaspoon vanilla
5 bananas
1 large can pineapple chunks
1 large non-dairy whipped topping

Mix maraschino cherries, chocolate syrup, nuts, graham crackers and butter mix and press into bottom of oblong pan. Mix cream cheese, sugar and vanilla. Spread onto crust mixture. Layer sliced bananas and pineapple chunks. Top with whipped topping. Sprinkle with nuts and cherries. Drizzle chocolate syrup over top. Refrigerate at least 5 hours.

Marilyn Van Ryn, Sacred Heart Cathedral Church, Knoxville, TN

Root Beer Float Ice Cream

1 egg
2 ¼ cups sugar
2 cups milk
2 cups half & half
4 cups whipping cream
½ teaspoon salt
2 ounces root beer concentrate
1 cup vanilla chips, finely chopped

In mixing bowl, beat egg. Gradually add sugar. Continue to beat with mixer until mixture is stiff. Add milk, half & half, whipping cream, salt, root beer concentrate, and vanilla chips. Mix thoroughly. Freeze.

John A. Medvigy, Kern County Fair,
Bakersfield, CA

Mom's Molasses Cookies

1 cup shortening
1 cup sugar
1 cup molasses
1 teaspoon salt
1 tablespoon nutmeg
1 teaspoon baking soda
½ cup hot water
Approximately 5 cups of flour

Preheat oven to 375°F. Cream shortening and sugar. Add molasses, salt, and nutmeg. Dissolve soda in hot water. Add to molasses mixture. Next add flour until ingredients are thoroughly mixed (only add enough flour to make it stiff enough to roll). Chill the dough. Roll dough into logs. Slice into ½-inch portions.

Grease cookie sheets. Place on cookie sheets. Bake about 8-10 minutes.

"This was originally my grandmother, Neta MacDaniel's recipe. Then my mom, Esther Wilson, used it and passed it down to me. So three generations have used this recipe."

Linda Brownell, Shady United Methodist Church, Shady, NY

Italian Cream Cake

<u>Cake</u>
1 stick butter (or margarine)
½ cup solid shortening
2 cups sugar
5 egg yolks
2 cups self-rising flour (add 1 teaspoon baking soda to flour)
1 cup buttermilk (may use regular milk)
1 teaspoon vanilla
1 ¼ cups coconut (optional)
1 cup chopped pecans
5 egg whites, stiffly beaten

<u>Frosting</u>
1 container (8-ounce) cream cheese
1 stick margarine
1 box confectioners' sugar
1 teaspoon vanilla

<u>For cake:</u> Preheat oven to 350°F. Cream butter and shortening. Add sugar beating until smooth. Add yolks. Beat well. Combine flour to cream mixture. Add buttermilk. Stir in vanilla and

coconut. Fold in egg whites. Pour into 3 round cake pans. Cook until toothpick comes out clean.

For frosting: Cream margarine and cream cheese until smooth. Add vanilla and sugar. Frost cake. Top with a sprinkling of chopped pecans.

Audrey Hinnant, Wilson County Fair,
Wilson, NC

Banana Cake & Brown Sugar Icing

<u>Banana Cake</u>
1 ½ cups sugar
½ cup margarine
2 eggs
4 tablespoons sour milk
4 mashed bananas
2 cups flour
Pinch of salt
1 teaspoon soda
1 cup chopped walnuts

<u>Brown Sugar Icing</u>
1 cup brown sugar
3 tablespoons milk
3 tablespoons margarine
1 tablespoon vanilla
1 box confectioners' sugar

<u>For cake:</u> Mix sugar, margarine and eggs. Add sour milk, then finely mashed bananas. Sift flour, salt and soda; add nuts & banana

mixture. Batter is runny. Bake for 45 minutes in 350°F oven in a large layer pan. Allow to cool, then top with brown sugar icing.

For icing: Bring first three ingredients to a boil. Let cool. Add vanilla. Add confectioners' sugar until it is of desired spreading consistency.

Nancy Mayuri, Bradley Rd. Missionary Baptist Church, Colorado Springs, CO

So Pretty In Pink

<u>Crust</u>
3 egg whites, room temperature
¼ teaspoons cream of tartar
⅛ teaspoon salt
Red food coloring
¾ cup sugar
½ teaspoon vanilla
½ cup pecan pieces, divided plus extra for garnish

<u>Filling</u>
1 package (8-ounce) cream cheese, softened
3 tablespoons solid butter flavored shortening
1 box (16-ounce) confectioners' sugar
1 can (15-ounce) sweet pitted cherries, chopped (use only about half)
½ cup maraschino cherries, chopped
Pecan pieces
1 carton (8-ounce) non-dairy whipped topping

Pre-heat oven 300°F. Grease a 9-inch non-stick pie pan with solid vegetable shortening or shortening spray. Dust thoroughly with flour. Set aside.

bowl, mix the buttermilk and vanilla. Slowly add flour a little at a time to the red paste mixture. Blend with mixer. When mixed thoroughly, add to batter. Thoroughly mix the vinegar and baking soda before adding to the batter. Hold it over the batter because it will foam up.

Bake in two 9-inch pans that have been sprayed with non-stick cooking spray. Test after 20 minutes for doneness. Cool completely on racks.

For icing: Mix the milk and flour in a pan on stove top and cook until stiff. Let cool until cold. Next, cream the butter, sugar and vanilla in a mixer. Add the milk and flour mixture and whip until desired consistency.

Note: It helps to have the beaters and glass-mixing bowl to be completely cold.

Gail Chandler, Sulphur Well Church of Christ,
Springville, TN

Country Pineapple Casserole

½ cup butter or margarine, softened
2 cups sugar
8 eggs
2 cans (20-ounce) crushed pineapple, drained
3 tablespoons lemon juice
10 slices day old white bread, cubed

Preheat oven to 325°F. In a mixing bowl, cream butter and sugar. Add eggs, one at a time, beating well after each addition. Stir in pineapple and lemon juice. Fold in the bread cubes. Pour into a greased 13x9x2-inch baking dish. Bake, uncovered for 35-40 minutes or until set. Yield: 12 to 16 servings.

Gale Foreshee, Kern County Fair,
Bakersfield, CA

Peanut Butter Cookies

3 cups flour
2 teaspoons soda
¼ teaspoon salt
1 cup solid shortening
2 eggs, beaten
1 cup sugar
1 cup brown sugar, packed
1 cup peanut butter (plain or chunky)
1 teaspoon vanilla

Preheat oven to 350°F. Sift flour once with soda and salt in a bowl. Set aside. Cream shortening, eggs, sugar, and brown sugar together until smooth. Add peanut butter. Stir well. Add flour mixture. Add vanilla and mix to a stiff batter. Form into tiny balls (¾-1-inch). Place on greased cookie sheet and press with a fork to make a waffle design. Bake for 8-10 minutes. Immediately remove from cookie sheets to cooling racks. Makes about 4 dozen 2 ½-inch cookies.

Cheryl Hudson, Kern County Fair,
Bakersfield, CA

Blue Ribbon Browned Butter Cream Cookies

<u>Cookie</u>
1 cup butter (no substitutes), softened
⅔ cup brown sugar, packed
2 egg yolks
½ teaspoon vanilla extract
2 ½ cups flour
⅓ cup finely chopped pecans
¼ teaspoon salt

<u>Filling</u>
2 tablespoons butter (no substitutes), plus 1 ½ teaspoons butter
1 ½ cups confectioners' sugar
½ teaspoon vanilla extract
2-3 tablespoons whipping cream

<u>For cookie</u>: Preheat oven to 350°F. In a mixing bowl, cream butter and brown sugar. Beat in egg yolks and vanilla. Combine flour, pecans, and salt. Gradually add to creamed mixture. Shape into two 10-inch rolls. Wrap each roll in plastic wrap. Refrigerate 1-2 hours. Unwrap and cut into ¼-inch slices. Place 2-inches

apart on ungreased baking sheets. Bake for 11-13 minutes or until golden brown. Remove and place on wire racks and cool.

For filling: Heat butter in saucepan over medium heat until golden brown. Remove from heat and add confectioners' sugar, vanilla, and enough cream until spreading consistency. Ice bottom half of cookies and top with remaining cookie. Makes about 3 dozen.

Betty Rutherford, Kern County Fair,
Bakersfield, CA

Blue Ribbon Blueberry Cheesecake

4 packages (2 pounds) cream cheese, softened
6 eggs
1 ½ cups sugar
3 tablespoons cornstarch
3 tablespoons flour
1 ½ tablespoons vanilla
1 tablespoon lemon juice
½ cup sour cream
1 cup whipping cream
¼ pound butter, melted (1 stick)
1 ¾ cups fresh or frozen blueberries
1 can (21-ounce) blueberry pie filling

Preheat oven to 350°F. In a bowl, combine cream cheese, eggs, sugar, cornstarch. Add flour, vanilla, and lemon juice. Blend in sour cream, whipping cream, butter, and blueberries. Pour into a buttered 10-inch springform pan. Bake for one hour. Turn oven off and allow cheesecake to cool for one hour in oven. Remove to a rack and cool completely. Preheat oven to 400°F.

Spread blueberry pie filling over top of cooled cheesecake. Bake for 15 minutes. Cool and refrigerate several hours before serving.

Betty Rutherford, Kern County Fair,
Bakersfield, CA

Lemon Sheet Cake

1 package (18 ¼-ounce) lemon cake mix
4 eggs
1 can (15 ¾-ounce) lemon pie filling
1 package (3-ounce) cream cheese, softened
½ cup butter, softened
2 cups confectioners' sugar
1 ½ teaspoons vanilla extract

For cake: Preheat oven to 350°F. In a large mixing bowl, beat the cake mix and eggs until well blended. Fold in pie filling. Spread into a greased 15x10x1-inch baking pan. Bake for 18-20 minutes or until a toothpick inserted near the center comes out clean. Cool on a wire rack.

For frosting: In a small bowl, beat cream cheese, butter, and powdered sugar until smooth. Stir in vanilla. Spread over cake. Store in the refrigerator.

Lillian O'Neal, Kern County Fair, Bakersfield, CA

"The Bomb"

2 ¾ cups Oreo® crumbs
½ cup melted unsalted butter
2 cups container heavy whipping cream
1 teaspoon vanilla extract
1 can (14-ounce) sweetened condensed milk
¼ cup sugar
2 teaspoons cornstarch
Large package frozen sliced strawberries in sugar
1 tablespoon fresh lemon juice

Combine crumbs and butter. Press 2 cups Oreo® mixture lightly into 9x13- inch pan. In a large bowl beat whipping cream and vanilla until soft peaks are formed. Fold sweetened condensed milk into mixture. Pour into pan. Freeze. Mix sugar and cornstarch in small bowl. Add large bowl with thawed strawberries and lemon juice. Pour over frozen whipped cream layer. Top with remaining crumb mixture and freeze for 6 hours.

Mary Alice Sain, Macedonia Baptist Church, Jackson TN

Blue Ribbon Apple Pie

<u>Crust</u>
Pinch of baking powder
½ teaspoon salt
2 ½ cups flour
2 sticks cold butter, cut into small pieces
6 tablespoons ice water

<u>Filling</u>
2 Gala apples
2 Golden Delicious apples
2 Granny Smith apples
1/6 cup cornstarch
1 cup sugar
1 teaspoon cinnamon
1 teaspoon lemon juice
2 tablespoons honey
Pinch of fresh nutmeg
1 tablespoon butter
1 tablespoon sugar
1 tablespoon butter, melted
1 tablespoon sugar

Preheat oven to 350°F.

<u>For crust</u>: Mix baking powder and salt into the flour. Add butter. Place into a food processor and process on pulse until butter is evenly distributed and mixture looks like cornmeal. Add 5 tablespoons of the ice water and let processor run until dough works itself into a ball. Add remaining tablespoon of water if necessary. Remove dough from processor. Divide into two equal balls and place on a piece of wax paper. Pat balls into a flat circle. Wrap up in wax paper. Refrigerate dough for 30 minutes before using.

<u>For filling</u>: Peel, core and cut apples into ½-inch slices. It should equal 8 cups of apples. Mix cornstarch, sugar and cinnamon thoroughly. Place apples in a large bowl and sprinkle with lemon juice. Mix in sugar mixture. Place filling in a prepared 9-inch pie pan. Drizzle with honey, sprinkle with nutmeg and dot with butter. Top with second crust and crimp edges to seal. Brush with the melted butter and sprinkle with 1 tablespoon sugar. Bake for 1 hour until crust is golden, the apples are tender and juices bubble.

Alicia Comstock Arter, Puyallup Fair, Puyallup, WA

Pumpkin Cake Roll

Cake Roll
3 eggs
1 cup sugar
⅔ cup pumpkin
1 teaspoon lemon juice
¾ cup flour
1 teaspoon baking powder
2 teaspoons cinnamon
1 teaspoon ginger
½ teaspoon nutmeg
½ teaspoon salt
1 cup finely chopped nuts

Filling
1 cup confectioners' sugar
4 tablespoons butter
2 packages (3-ounces each) cream cheese
½ teaspoon vanilla

For cake roll: Preheat oven to 375°F. Beat eggs on high speed for 5 minutes. Gradually beat in sugar. Stir in pumpkin and lemon juice. Mix the dry ingredients and fold into pumpkin mixture. Spread in greased and floured 15x10x1-inch pan. Top with chopped nuts. Bake for 15 minutes. Turn out on towel, sprinkled with confectioners' sugar. Starting at narrow end, roll towel and cake together. Cool. Unroll and spread filling over entire cake surface. Re-roll cake. Chill.

For filling: Combine all ingredients. Beat until smooth. Place on top of cake.

Marsha Allen, Kern County Fair,
Bakersfield, CA

Banana Split Dessert

2 cups graham cracker crumbs
1 stick unsalted butter, melted
2 eggs
2 sticks unsalted butter
2 cups confectioners' sugar
4 large bananas, sliced
1 can pineapple tidbits, drained
1 container non-dairy whipped topping
Maraschino cherries
Chocolate syrup
Chopped pecans, optional

Put graham crackers in food processor. Pulse until crumbs are like powder. Add melted butter. Pulse. Put into 9x13-inch pan.

In large mixing bowl, add eggs, butter, and confectioners' sugar. Mix for 15-20 minutes (any less and mixture will separate). Pour over crumbs. Slice bananas and press into mixture. Layer pineapple over bananas. Spread whipped topping over pineapple. Add maraschino cherries, drizzle with chocolate syrup. Sprinkle with pecans if desired. Chill and serve. Also freezes well.

Mary Alice Sain, Macedonia Baptist Church,
Jackson TN

Pecan Caramel Bars

1 package vanilla wafers, crushed
2 tablespoons sugar
¾ cup butter or margarine, melted
1 can sweetened condensed milk
1 egg
½ teaspoon maple flavoring
1 cup butterscotch chips
1 ½ cups coarsely chopped pecans

Preheat oven to 350°F. Combine wafer crumbs, sugar and butter. Press into greased 13x9-inch baking pan. Bake for 8-10 minutes. Cool for 10 minutes.

In a small bowl, beat condensed milk, egg and maple flavoring. Stir in butterscotch chips. Spread over crust. Sprinkle with pecans. Bake for 20-22 minutes. Cool. Cut into bars. Yield 3 dozen.

Dortha Reinhart, DeKalb County Fair, Butler, IN

Peanut Butter Ice Cream Topping

1 cup brown sugar, packed
⅓ cup milk
¼ cup light corn syrup
1 tablespoon butter
½ cup peanut butter

In medium saucepan, combine brown sugar, milk, corn syrup, and butter. Cook over medium heat, stirring constantly, until sugar is dissolved and butter is melted. Remove from heat. Add peanut butter. Beat with mixer until smooth. Pour over ice cream while warm.

Helen Henson, Kern County Fair,
Bakersfield, CA

White Chocolate Truffle and Chocolate Fudge Layer Cake

Cake
4 ounces unsweetened chocolate, chopped
1 ¾ cups all-purpose flour
¼ cup unsweetened cocoa powder
1 teaspoon baking powder
¾ teaspoon baking soda
½ teaspoon salt
2 cups sugar
½ cup unsalted butter
2 teaspoons vanilla
2 large eggs
1 ½ cups whole milk

Filling and Frosting
3 cups whipping cream
¼ cup butter
1 pound white chocolate, finely chopped
2 teaspoons vanilla extract
½ teaspoon almond extract
4 tablespoons amaretto
Chocolate stars, optional (see page 243)

<u>For cake</u>: Preheat oven to 350°F. Melt chopped chocolate in saucepan. Cool. Sift flour, cocoa powder, baking powder, baking soda, and salt. Cream sugar and butter. Add cooled, melted unsweetened chocolate and vanilla. Add eggs, 1 at a time. Mix in cocoa powder mixture, alternating with milk. Pour batter in two 9-inch prepared cake pans and bake for 35 minutes. Cool for 10 minutes. Turn cakes out on racks.

<u>For filling</u>: Simmer 1 cup cream and butter over medium heat. Remove from heat and add white chocolate; stir until smooth. Whisk in vanilla; pour 1 ½ cups of white chocolate filling into small bowl. Cover and freeze until cold (about 2 hours).

<u>For frosting</u>: Beat remaining 2 cups cream and almond extract until peaks form. Fold in remaining lukewarm white chocolate mixture. Refrigerate for 3 hours.

Brush 2 tablespoons amaretto over top of each cake layer. Spread chilled 1 ½ cups white chocolate filling over bottom layer. Top with second cake. Spread whipped cream frosting over top and sides of cake. Refrigerate for 1 hour. Arrange chocolate stars decoratively on top of cake. Serve.

Rosalyn B. Collier, Kern County Fair, Bakersfield, CA

Chocolate Italian Cream Cake with Cocoa Cream Cheese Frosting

Cake
½ cup solid vegetable shortening
½ cup butter
2 cups sugar
5 eggs, yolks and whites separated
2 cups flour
1 teaspoon baking soda
¼ cup cocoa
1 cup buttermilk
1 cup walnuts, chopped
1 cup coconut
1 teaspoon vanilla
White chocolate for garnish

Frosting
1 cup butter, softened
1 container (8-ounce) cream cheese
8 cups confectioners' sugar
1 cup cocoa
2 teaspoons vanilla
1 cup walnuts, chopped

For cake: Preheat oven to 350°F. Grease and flour four 9-inch cake pans. Cream shortening and butter until fluffy. Gradually add sugar. Beat well. Add yolks, one at a time. Beat well after each addition. Sift flour, soda, and cocoa. Add to creamed mixture alternately with buttermilk. Begin and end with flour mixture. Stir in nuts, coconut and vanilla. Beat egg whites until stiff. Fold into batter. Pour evenly into pans and bake for 20-25 minutes. Cool. Ice with Cocoa Cream Cheese Frosting. Decorate with white chocolate.

For frosting: Cream butter and cream cheese. Beat until fluffy. Add sugar, cocoa powder, and vanilla. Blend on low until moistened. Beat on medium until fluffy. Fold in nuts.

Kelly B. Everhart, Best of Show, Florida State Fair

Upside Down Caramel Apple Pie

<u>Crust</u>
3 cups flour
¾ teaspoon salt
1 cup solid shortening
1 egg
1 teaspoon vinegar
7-10 tablespoons cold water

<u>Glaze:</u>
¼ cup packed brown sugar
1 tablespoon butter, melted
1 tablespoon light corn syrup
½ cup pecan halves

<u>Filling:</u>
5 large Granny Smith apples, sliced thinly
1 tablespoon lemon juice
½ cup brown sugar, packed
3 tablespoons flour
Dash ground nutmeg
¾ teaspoon cinnamon
1 cup prepared caramel dipping sauce

For crust: Mix flour and salt, cut in shortening until texture resembles cornmeal. In separate bowl, mix egg, vinegar and water. Add liquid to flour mixture and toss gently with fork. Divide dough into halves and form balls. Roll out on lightly floured surface.

Preheat oven to 425°F.

For glaze: Combine brown sugar, melted butter, and corn syrup. Spread evenly on the bottom of a 9-inch glass pie plate. Arrange pecan halves on top of glaze in a pattern around the dish (circle). Top with one pastry crust, and set aside.

For filling: Take sliced apples and toss in lemon juice. In large skillet cook apples until tender, about 10 minutes. In medium bowl mix brown sugar, flour, nutmeg, cinnamon, set aside. Take ½ of the cooked apples and put on pastry crust that was set aside. Then sprinkle with ½ of the flour/brown sugar mixture and ½ of the caramel dipping sauce. Add rest of the apples, then sprinkle with flour/brown sugar mixture and remaining caramel sauce. Add remaining pastry crust over the top of apples. Fold edges under bottom of crust and flute edges. Cut slits in top of crust to vent. Bake 50-60 minutes or until golden brown. Take out of oven and let stand for 5 minutes. Loosen edges from pie plate and invert onto a heatproof plate or dish. Scrape any caramel and put on top of pie. Cool one hour before serving.

Heidi Neidlinger, Gratz Fair & Pennsylvania Farm Show,
Gratz, PA / Harrisburg, PA

Chocolate Strawberry Cake

<u>Cake</u>
3 cups all purpose flour
1 ½ cups cocoa
4 ½ teaspoons baking soda
¼ teaspoon salt
3 cups sugar
3 eggs
1 ½ cups vegetable oil
1 teaspoon vanilla
3 cups warm water
1 ⅓ cups strawberry jam, divided

<u>Cream Filling</u>
5 tablespoons flour
1 cup milk
1 stick margarine
½ cup shortening
1 cup sugar
¼ teaspoon salt
1 teaspoon vanilla

<u>Butter Cream Frosting</u>
½ cup butter

9 tablespoons cocoa with 3 tablespoons melted butter
4 cups confectioners' sugar
2 teaspoons vanilla
3 tablespoons milk

For cake: Heat oven to 350°F. Grease and flour bottom of 3 round cake pans. In large bowl, whisk together flour, cocoa, baking soda and salt until blended. In another large bowl, beat sugar and eggs on medium speed for 1 minute. Add oil and vanilla, beating until combined. Add flour mixture in 3 parts alternating with water, beginning and ending with flour mixture; beat just until combined. Pour evenly into pans. Bake 35-40 minutes or until toothpick inserted in centers comes out clean. Cool pans on wire rack for 10 minutes. Invert onto wire racks. Cool completely. Place one layer on serving plate, spread with ⅔ cup strawberry jam. Top with 1 cup cream filling. Top second cake layer with ⅔ cup strawberry jam and 1 cup cream filling. Top with remaining cake layer. Frost top and sides with butter cream frosting.

For cream filling: Cook flour and milk until thick, stirring constantly. Cool. Cream other ingredients and add cooked flour mixture one tablespoon at a time.

For butter cream frosting: Beat all ingredients in a large bowl until light and fluffy.

Kiwanis Wyoming County Fair, Meshopen, PA

Chocolate Stars for White Chocolate Truffle and Chocolate Fudge Layer Cake

6 ounces bittersweet chocolate, chopped
1 tablespoon solid vegetable shortening
Nonstick vegetable spray

Melt chocolate and shortening in double boiler until melted and smooth. Pour onto foil baking sheet, spreading mixture evenly. Refrigerate about 12 minutes. Spray assorted star-shaped cookie cutters. Cut out stars. Refrigerate until firm, about 30 minutes; transfer to foil lined cookie sheet and refrigerate until ready to use. Arrange Chocolate Stars decoratively on top of cake and serve.

Rosalyn B. Collier, Kern County Fair,
Bakersfield, CA

Contributors

Alexander, Chad
Alexander, Kelly
Alexander, Michael
Allen, Marsha
Anderson, Jeanine Mower
Ard, Holly
Arter, Alicia Comstock
Babb, Lois
Ballew, Joyce
Bartholomew, Carol
Blackford, Sherry
Blair, Sabrina
Blizzard, Mike
Boesendahl, Maryellen
Boggs, Richard
Brackins, Dorothy
Brackins, Joseph D.
Brackins, Mom & Dad
Broadbent, Annie
Brownell, Linda
Buchannon, Gladys
Bullock, Robin
Cate, Zelma
Chandler, Gail
Collier, Rosalyn B.
Coombs, Cynthia
Costanza, Amy
Cottrell, Judy
Cumm, Shana
Dennison, Rachel
Deyton, Julia

Dotson, Buena
Dotson-Wooley, Linda
Drake, Mrs. James
Duvall, Kenneth L.
Eckler, Phyllis
Edwards, Alice
Elbirn, John
Everhart, Kelly B.
Farmer, Warnita
Fensermaker, Audra
Fidler, Jane
Fingers, Roy
Foreshee, Gale
Francka, Barbara
Franzetta, Rachel
Goldstein, Joanne
Goodale, Lisa
Gooden, Ella
Gregson, Bobby
Gregson, Gay
Griesbaum, Jill
Griesbaum, Sophia
Grooms, Anita
Hamblen, Betty
Hampgaard, Anna
Hancock, Dana
Hardin, Mary & Enoch
Harris, Kathy
Hathon, Stacey
Hays, Lisa
Heath, Judy
Hendrickson, Jolynn
Henson, Helen
Higgins, Pat
Hill, Sandra
Hinnant, Audrey
Holmes, Elizabeth
Hudson, Cheryl
Hull, Anne
Hull, Jeff & Henri
Hull, Valerie
Jarvis, Barbara

Jones, Angie
Jones, David
Kressig, Betty
Kuhner, Mary Ann
Livingstone, David
Loftis, Olivia
Madden, Brenda L.
Madden, Helen
Madden, James
Mary (Melanie's Mom)
Mayuri, Nancy
McDade, Paul
McKnight, Kay
McKnight, Melissa
McKnight, Wendy
McLeary, Mary
Medvigy, John A.
Mitchell, Petra
Meredith, Shirley M.
Mitchell, Shirley E.
Mitchell, Susie
Moore, Dottie
Morris, Gary
Murphy, Anna
Murhpy, Calvin Jr.
Murphy, Josephine
Murphy, Libby
Neidlinger, Heidi
Odell, Diane
O'Neal, Lillian
Parton, Floyd
Parton, Stella
Payne, Ethel
Peace, Ben
Peck, Colleen
Pederson, Mary Beth
Peek, Jill
Peek, Louise
Peterson, Ramona
Profit, Bekky
Profit, Sean
Profit, Jolynn

Profit, Scott
Profit, Vicky
Ramey, Liz
Rauhoff, Tim
Reid, Lady Sheila
Reinhart, Dortha
Reynolds, Bob & Becky
Rob & Cathy
Roberson, Rodney K.
Roderer, Marci & Keziah
Rutherford, Betty
Sain, Mary Alice
Sanchez, Rosa & Marisela
Satkowski, Tricia
Schwank, Liz
Scott, Buddy
Scott, Sandra
Scott, Sylvia
Sharp. Alan
Shaw, Edna
Shelton, John
Shimota, John
Simmons, Roy
Smithyman, Linda
Snawder, Joan
Spargo, John
Summer, Donna
Taylor, Alice
Taylor, Glen
Taylor, Joe
Taylor, Mae
Tener, Renee
Thomas, Mike
Topping, Beth
Tripp, Judy & Charlie
Urbanek, Julia
Van Ryn, Marilyn
Van Ryn, Trudy
Watson, Ben & Kim
Weatherby, Betty
White, Dee
White, Jason

White, Susan
White, Tim
White, Todd
White, Trisha
Williams, Natalie (Mickey)
Wisse, Larry & Brenda
Woods, Renae
Young, Debbie
Young, Jeannie
Young, Kristi
Young, Randy
Young, Wayne
Youngblood, Bonnie
Zarrillo, Carmela
Zealer, David

Credits

Index

4-H Special	87
5 Layer Bars	254
5 Minute Crockpot Burritos	106
Angel Food Cake	220
Aunt Helen's Red Velvet Cake	276
Baked Beans	136
Baked or Grilled Potatoes	162
Baked Tomato Wedges	135
Banana Cake	272
Banana Frost	14
Banana Split Cake	266
Banana Split Dessert	290
Bar-B-Que	127
Basic White Bread	62
Beef Tips	130
Beef Stew	74
Best Pecan Pie Ever	228
Biscuits	49
Black-Eyed Peas	154
Blue Ribbon Apple Pie	286
Blue Ribbon Blueberry Cheesecake	282
Blueberry Sour Cream Corn Muffins	38
Blueberry Muffins	54
Breakfast Squares	95
Broccoli Casserole	144
Broccoli with Rice	159
Browned Butter Cream Cookies	280
Butter Fried Carrots	158
Buttery Crunch Topped Tomatoes	146
Cabbage Salad	84
Cabbage Soup	79
Cabbage Stew	148
Cajun Grilled Chicken	131
Candied Yams	161
Caramel Apple Cheesecake	204
Caramel Icing	247
Caramel Pudding	229

Caramel-Pecan-Pretzel Candies	250
Carrot Muffins	258
Carrot Pudding	246
Chardonnay Pork	122
Charleston Coconut Pie	251
Cheesy Ranch Potato Bake	168
Chess Cake Bars	248
Chicken Almond Salad	70
Chicken Cheese Chowder	77
Chicken Enchilada Bake	100
Chicken Pot Pie	104
Chicken Puffs	110
Chicken Stir-Fry	115
Chili Chili, Bang Bang!	120
Chili Chili	126
Chili Dog Pie	101
Chinese Chicken	98
Chocolate Bread Pudding	196
Chocolate Bread Pudding	198
Chocolate Italian Cream Cake	296
Chocolate Pie	253
Chocolate Pumpkin Cookies	234
Chocolate Sop Gravy	201
Chocolate Stars	302
Chocolate Strawberry Cake	300
Cinnamon Apple Muffins	35
Cinnamon Apple Muffins	58
Cinnamon Candy	257
Cinnamon Rolls	46
Coal Black Cake	222
Coca-Cola® Roast	107
Cocoa Drop Cookies	209
Coconut Cream Pie	224
Copper Pennies	147
Corn Sauté	150
Country Bacon Green Beans	166
Country Pineapple Casserole	278
Cranberry Bread	50
Cranberry Orange Punch	15
Cranberry Salad	75
Cranberry Tea	19
Cream Cheese Pie	208

Creamed Sweet Potatoes — 156
Creamsicle Jell-O® — 200
Creamy Pea Salad — 76
Croutons — 36
Crusty Garlic Bread — 39
Crusty Lamb Chops — 116
Delicious Pork Chops — 108
Delicious Stuffed Squash — 151
Divinity — 218
Dump Cake — 219
Dutch Meatloaf — 99
Easy Hot Rolls — 42
Eggplant Parmesan — 164
Elegant Crab Soup — 78
French Toast — 48
Fried Chicken — 113
Fried Green Tomatoes — 142
Fried Rice — 178
Fruit Juice Cooler — 16
Fruited Flank Steak — 112
Garlic-Buttered Noodles — 180
German Chocolate Pound Cake — 205
German Potato Salad — 137
Gob Cake — 212
Golden Pasta Exotica — 184
Gorgonzola — 102
Graham Cracker Cookies — 249
Grand Champion Sponge Cake — 223
Granny's Green Jell-O® Salad — 91
Green Bean Casserole — 152
Grilled Vegetable Kabobs — 153
Hash Brown Casserole — 155
Herbed Corn on the Cob — 141
Hot Fudge Pudding Cake — 230
Hot Garlic & Anchovy Dip — 23
Hush Puppies — 45
Ice Cream Sandwich Cake — 252
Irish Potato Salad — 86
Iron Skillet Biscuits — 41
Iron Skillet Cornbread — 33
Italian Cream Cake — 270
Italian Style Potatoes — 163

Jalapeño Cornbread 44
Jalapeño Wheat Cheese Rolls 26
Keebler® Fudge Stick Cookie Cake 244
Lemon Hearts with Butter Crust 202
Lemon Sheet Cake 284
Lemonade 13
Macaroni & Cheese Pie 187
Macaroni & Cheese 181
Macaroni Ring 182
Mae's Apple Pie 193
Mandarin Marshmallow Salad 81
Marinated Cheese 30
Meatballs Royale 125
Melt-A-Ways 264
Mexican Bean Dip 21
Mixed Berry Pie 242
Mom's Molasses Cookies 268
Most Delicious Rolls 34
Oilolio 177
Old Fashioned Slaw 89
Old South Bread Pudding 194
Onion or Cheddar Bread 59
Orange Glow Cheesecake 232
Oriental Salad 73
Party Bean Dip 25
Pasta Primavera 183
Peanut Butter Cookies 279
Peanut Butter Ice Cream Topping 293
Pecan Caramel Bars 292
Pecan Squares 256
Pecan-Coated Fried Crappie 96
PennyWise Skillet Supper Dish 124
Pineapple Peach Star Upside Down Cake 236
Pineapple Pie 255
Pineapple Surprise 216
Praline Wafer Dessert 210
Pumpkin Cake Roll 288
Pumpkin Raisin Muffins 65
Ramen Noodles Salad 82
Raspberry Chocolate Mousse Cups 260
Raw Cranberry Salad 88
Raw Vegetable Salad 83

RazzCherry Pie	238
Red White & Blue Cake	214
Rice Casserole	176
Roast Rib of Beef Au Jus	118
Root Beer Float Ice Cream	267
Rum Cakes	262
Rustic Lasagna	185
Salsa Reynolds	28
Sausage Jambalaya	97
Savory Sausage Shells	128
Scones	64
Slap 'Yo Momma Spaghetti	188
Smokin' Salsa	29
So Pretty In Pink	274
South of the Border Cornbread Bake	60
Southern Cracklin' Bread	37
Southern Sweet Potato Casserole	170
Southwest Vegetable Dip	24
Spaghetti Crust Pie	175
Spaghetti Sauce	186
Spamtacular Sunnydogs	114
Sparkling Harves Cider	18
Spinach Salad	90
Spotted Seasoned Snakes	56
Stir-Fry Vegetables with Sausage	165
Strawberry Banana Shortcake	217
Strawberry Pretzel Salad	72
Summer Salad	80
Sweet Potato Cobbler	195
Sweet Potato Pudding	138
Swiss Fondue	22
Tennessee Pudding	226
"The Bomb"	285
Tomato Juice Bread	52
Tomato Supreme	145
Tortilla Rolls	160
Tri Tip Roast	117
Tripp Tater Salad	167
Tropical Dream Pie	240
Trudy's German Potato Salad	169
Upside Down Caramel Apple Pie	298
Vegetable Dip	20

Vegetable Soup 69
Vegetarian Baked Beans 140
Veggie Bars 40
Wassail 17
White Chocolate Blackberry Cheesecake 206
White Chocolate Truffle and Chocolate Fudge Layer Cake 294
Zucchini Bake 149

About the Author

Stella is a consummate entertainer and a true song stylist. She has touched audiences worldwide not only through her music, but her stage, television, and film presence as well.

Stella began her entertainment career at an early age singing gospel music with her family — in church and on television and radio. Her first two albums, which included several original compositions, reflected that early influence and delivered that same sincerity and honesty which is felt in her music today.

She has recorded 28 chart singles, 19 albums and garnered numerous awards and nominations. She is a frequent guest on major television shows across America, Great Britain, Scandinavia, Europe and Australia.

Stella took on the rigors of the theatre, starring in four New York touring productions, including Seven Brides for Seven Brothers,

The Best Little Whorehouse In Texas, Pump Boys and Dinettes, and Gentlemen Prefer Blondes. She has been featured in such films as "Cloud Dancer," "The Loner" and "Country Gold." Her work in television has included "The Dukes of Hazzard" and the CBS-TV movie, "The Color of Love," co-starring Lou Gossett, Jr. and Gena Rowlands.

But entertainment is not the only area where Stella shines. She devotes much of her time to causes such as battered women and children's shelters and stamping out poverty in the Appalachian region.

Stella's desire and ability to relate to people from all walks of life, coupled with her diverse talents, are qualities that have made her one of America's richest musical treasures.

www.stellaparton.com

P.O. Box 120871
Nashville, TN 37212